The Emerald Scroll

The Nameless Path Beyond

Doshema

Edited by James L Bailey

Spirit Ascension - 2023

Spirit Ascension Publishing
Toronto, Ontario, Canada M4Y2J4

ISBN 978-1-7774618-2-9

© 2023 by James L. Bailey

All rights reserved. No part of this publication may be reproduced, distributed, or transmitted in any form or by any means, including photocopying, recording, or other electronic or mechanical methods, without the prior written permission of the publisher, except in the case of brief quotations embodied in critical reviews and certain other non-commercial uses permitted by copyright law. For permission requests, contact publisher: Doshema@gmail.com

Cover designed by DOSHEMA

Contents

BOOK ONE

The Emerald Scroll
The Nameless Path Beyond

1.	The Bell Rings, the Mind Whispers, the Mirror Reflects	11
2.	The Architect's Labyrinth	30
3.	Entering the Temple of Initiation	57
4.	Shadow embrace, Osiris is Resurrected	75
5.	Dril-bu & Dorje United	79

BOOK TWO

Artificially Intelligent Time
The Heartbeat of an Ancient God

1.	Contemplation	93
2.	Binary Reproductive Flesh	102
3.	Mysterium Coniunectionis	108
4.	Eternal Return	117
5.	Erebus Awakens	124
6.	Star of Babylon	136

7. Emerald Revelation — 145

BOOK THREE

Beyond The Sphere of Destiny
In Out Around

THE WAY IN

1.	Samsara	171
2.	The Black Square	173
3.	The Lovers Curse	177
4.	The Desert Wheel	178
5.	Fertile Ground	180
6.	Legion	182
7.	In His Image	184
8.	Viscera	187
9.	Daoist Tantra	188
10.	The Thorn Crown	191
11.	Freedom	193
12.	Adam's Equal	194
13.	The Corrupt Seed	198
14.	Church Upon the Hill	202
15.	The Babylonian Moth	204
16.	Phoenix	206
17.	Childhood Blood Allegiance	207
18.	The Wandering Fool	211

19. Red Skies in The Morning	212
20. Disciple 2:16	214
21. Infiltrator	219

THE WAY OUT

1. The Ghost in The Machine	224
2. The Parasite of Perception	229
3. The Dragons Den	247
4. Forced Worship	250
5. House Of Sorrow	251
6. Reverse The Fields	253
7. The Hero's Sacrifice	256
8. Solid State Ignorance	259
9. Reflection	260
10. Geometry	264
11. The Cave	265
12. Silk Portal	270
13. The Conductor	271
14. The Sacrifice of Fire	273
15. Selfless Hand	275
16. Questionable Value	277
17. Zero	278
18. Coincidental Space for Time	280
19. Throne of Destiny	287

THE WAY AROUND

1. Ouroboros	291
2. The Grigori	293
3. The Fourth Circle	296
4. Revelation	299
5. Eternal Return	302

6.	11:28:15	304
7.	Vav	306
8.	The Ninth Hour	308
9.	The Black Sun	310
10.	Thelema	313

BEYOND

1.	Pratyeka Yana	316
2.	Primordial Lotus	322
3.	The Thrice Greatest	325
4.	The Fruitless Season	333

APPENDICES

Form and Number	338
The Sun's Chariot	343

BOOK ONE

The Emerald Scroll

The Nameless Path Beyond

The Bell Rings, the Mind Whispers, the Mirror Reflects.

Doshema. Strange to me still,
is this connection or attachment (1)
that contradictively binds me through
division to this conceptual idea of wholeness.

Could it be that "I" am the very Void holding
my existence together? Or, is the dissolution of (2)
the shadow's grip upon the shores of attachment,
the means of escape or Way to Freedom?

Teacher. The actions of holding and releasing
are both bound to the same fate, the fate of all (3)
actions, the fate of Action itself.

Action is Form in Motion, and Motion is the eternal (4)
Cause and Effect of all Existential Form.

Grasping is the Cause, and releasing becomes the
Effect, and vice versa successionally. (5)

The transition between states of any kind is, (6)
of course, only possible through motion.

All "Things" or acts of definement are subject
to motion; without movement, "no-thing" would (7)
be seemingly definable nor thus come into existence.

Reflection. So, how does one escape motion?
How does one dissolve the Void or the definably (8)
separate parts its presence manifests?

This question also raises the inquiry as to why (9)
one would wish to escape the human condition.

Doshema. Sitting within the Hermetic temporal
chamber of silent contemplation, I witness the (10)
cyclically repetitious rise and fall of the primal
life-sustaining, breath-like tide of creative
destruction.

In the creational distance,
I perceive a child transform into an adult
through the cocoon of space-time, (11)
but unlike the caterpillar that emerges from its
magical veil as a beautiful butterfly,
the child is rewarded not with elevating wings
of freedom, but with the terrestrial suffering
of old Age and the gravitational pull of Saturn.

As a silent witness of the human condition,
I perceive all motion stemming forth from one
covertly planted creative seed hidden beneath   (12)
the surface soil of ignorance within the creative
chemical chaos released from the Pandoric Abyss.

Teacher. The breath is the unseen Triune essence
of Life within the human condition, not merely
on a dualistic converging elemental energetic   (13)
level–Blood, but also on an atomic vibrational
form structuring Pythagorean conscious intelligence
level– Space-Time-Awareness.

Again, we see Cause and Effect in action;
the Cause being the inward holding of the   (14)
oxygenated Inhalation, and the Effect is the
Outward carbon dioxide releasing exhalation of breath.

Like the triangle or symbolic pyramid,
the Apex is the transitional point between   (15)
the rise and fall of all motion-Life.

That being said,
this would suggest that the Shadow is   (16)
the Void from which Cause and Effect
come into being.

The Apex is Awareness,
the Cause is space, and the Effect is time,   (17)
remembering that space and time are One
beyond the ignorance of the shadow.

The human being is unaware that its very
existence is relatively caught between two   (18)
destructive forces: the Inhalation's implosive
force and the exhalation's explosive force.

The breath is very powerful,
and this insight might bring a new   (19)
understanding of the practice of Pranayama.

Reflection. If the Apex or transitional point is
the creator or vessel from which Cause and   (20)
Effect come into being, and ignorance in motion
is a characteristic of the Shadow, does this mean
that Awareness is centred in the Void?

Teacher. The human condition is subject to the
laws of the breath, which facilitates its existence.   (21)

The Body has two basic systems of action,   (22)
just like the breath. It has an open system that
acts as a funnel and a closed system that acts
as a pump.

The interactive dimensions of the Body are
Within and *Without–Electromagnetic.*   (23)
The Mind's dimension, the Apex of the
dual Body is *Around–Neutral.*

These are, of course, the three dimensions of a sphere; Within/Magnetic, Without/Electric and Around/Electromagnetic. (24)

Teacher. The *in-out* open Funnel system function of the body, which is also reflected in the Mind, is in relation to Space and Time. (25)

What goes in must come out; this is the relative convergence of energy. (26)

This is the natural flow of the universe in balance or order; only the ignorance of gross and subtle attachment disrupts this balance and initiates the process of chaos in the form of mental and physical disease. (27)

The Funnel within the body is the *Line* between the mouth and anus, and within the brain, the corpus callosum, which connects the right hemisphere to the left hemisphere, and within the subtle Mind, the transitional space-time between subconscious potential manifestation and conscious manifestation. (28)

The Funnel function of the body can be geometrically represented as a Line– that which gives positionality to two definable points of reference. (29)

Reflection. This would suggest that when the body
or mind holds onto something within past the point
of its usefulness, be it mental thoughts or physical (30)
nourishment, that which it covets becomes a
poisonous attachment that spawns the infectious
disease of Chaos—within the Mind and Body.

This would also suggest that the geometric
Line makes the open system possible and is (31)
the cause/effect of all desirous suffering
through its relational attachment to
positional definement.

Teacher. The *circulative* Pump closed system
function of the body, which is also reflected in (32)
the Mind, is in relation to Samsara.

The Ouroboros,
the Serpent which bends the Line (33)
of Time to create a Space
in which to form an infinite Circle.

Blood is the currency of human existence;
flesh is the object of obsession upon which (34)
it is spent.

It is the circular current which manifests the
friction of rhythm, and it is from this rhythm (35)
that Matter takes form.

As above, so as below, or as in the Macrocosm,
so as in the Microcosm. (36)

That which stimulates and regulates the current of
Life into motion, or that which manifests experience
through the inspiration of desire, is the Heart of all (37)
Matter at the center of all non-existent existence—the
Head of the Great Serpent.

Reflection. This could suggest that the Heart and
Serpent are symbolically one, both symbolizing (38)
desire through the circulation of the Life current.

Could this be the central esoteric key of the
exoteric religious and pagan mystery? (39)

Doshema. At the center of the desirous
fleshy fruit of which all ignorant sentient (40)
beings lust after, slumbers a sacred seed
within the selfish embrace of a maternal
parasitic material shell.

Unborn within the enchanted womb of (41)
the shadow, awaits the imprisoned spark
of awakening.

Teacher. The philosophy of oneness,
when applied physically, is a dangerous tool (42)
in the hands of predominately egocentric nations.

It is oppressive in its repetitive function,
breaking down self-identity through conformative
 hypnosis, only to replace it with servitude compliant (43)
to the authoritarian's source of power physically
manifested into form.

The art of Influence is a mastered skill within (44)
the arsenal of the center of power.

Curious or enlightening to some,
is the origin of this art, (45)
that being Astrologically based and thus ethereally
connected to the celestial spheres or Stars of Destiny.

Mythologically speaking,
the celestial realm is the abode of the Gods, (46)
the fashioners of humankind and imprinters
of Purpose directed and propelled by the
ignorance of Desire.

The Magick of Influence is archaic, (47)
ancient, and thus time-tested as a powerful
device of manipulative control through chaos and order.

Good and Evil are only constructs of infinite (48)
subjective measure and, therefore, truly undefinable.

Reflection. So, what is the reward for vice or virtue?
Where does pleasure transition into pain? (49)
In essence, where does the finite separate from
the infinite?

There are, of course, two forms of Influence; (50)
direct and Indirect—simply, known and unknown.

Doshema. Do I uplift him, (51)
let her fall, or allow the child to remain unborn?

This geometric triune realm forces the circle to
become a square, (52)
and still,
they seek freedom through its measure.

A lustful rage lingers deep only to surface (53)
in unfulfilled disgust.

The smell,
taste,
touch, (54)
sight,
and sound are a disappointing
reality to their delusional pleasure-producing thoughts.

How was this conscience formed that now subjects (55)
me to suffer the consequences of action and inaction?

A continuous burn that only the senses distract
you from, with but another form of suffering (56)
composed of ignorance.

I am tired yet again, or maybe the Arcane Chariot (57)
Wheel is once again pushing me into the alchemical
soil as it moves towards judgment.

Teacher. One must substitute Compassion for Rage,
for rage is a venomous poison which circulates (58)
through the mind infecting one's thoughts and
body constitution, with debilitating disease.

The Serpent's dual fangs bite and inject the
venom of ignorance into the One, (59)
which binds the mind to the body as separate entities.

Through this ignorance, Division comes into being, (60)
and from this division, the Square of measure is born.

He is the Body, and She is the Mind;
to Raise one is to Lower the other;
this is the essence of measurement, (61)
the existential "Scales" of infinite suffering
cycling from the Womb to the Tomb.

The Senses are the great distractors of this truth, (62)
tempting the clarity of One-pointedness into the
chaotic confusion of measure's endless divisible nature.

Reflection. The Chariot is symbolic of the human
experience of travelling through space-time between (63)
Life and Death.

The charioteer is the Mind that holds the reins of (64)
attention connected to the animal senses.

At the same time, the chariot itself is the
Body which houses the mind, (65)
which is directed by desire, and
propelled through Judgement.

In order to make a judgement,
there must be at least two different points
of reference beyond the Judge, hence (66)
the configuration of the court of law,
which separates the two parties;
prosecution and defence before the judge.

Like a game played on a "court," the motion
moves from one side to the other, refereed at (67)
the center by an impartial judge traditionally
dressed in Black and White.

Motion is governed by "Law," (68)
for Judgement is the predetermined fate of all action.

This is why the planetary god Saturn is the (69)
ruler of Law,
Time and Death,
for the fate of all human beings moving through
the mental and physical laws of space-time…is Death.

Doshema. Purpose for the purposeless;
I witness them crawl, walk and limp in search (70)
of Its illusional fulfillment and salvational attainment.

In understanding,
I embrace the Eternally tormented Nietzsche
caught within the universal web of Return, (71)
for I, too,
have witnessed the Babylonian Black
Widow of despairing knowledge at the subtle
center of the philosopher's endless pursuit of meaning.

Flesh and Bone,
Life and Death;
paradoxically unwarily bound to the same (72)
existential fate, the destiny of Blood, which
illusorily separates the One into two with the
deceptive mirage of Choice.

Teacher. Purpose is a sadistically masochistic (73)
killer disguised as a smiling,
attention-seeking child luring clown.

The human condition is subject to (74)
objective reality, and all subjectivity
is inspired by objective form.

This means that the subject and object are one,
for one cannot exist without the other within
the Human condition; (75)
relatively speaking,
the "Cause" of one becomes the "Effect" of
the other and vice versa.

Purpose,
in essence, is to fulfill the Functions for which (76)
the Form was created– Form denotes Function.

There is only One constant within the Human (77)
condition or consciously perceivable existence,
and that is Change.

All subjective and objective manifestation is
transient or impermanent,
and thus but a mirage, (78)
an enchantment
conjured by the Necromancer of Time.

Doshema. Teacher! (79)
Listen in silence,
remembering that you, too,
are always a student of Reflection.

I will speak below the poetry of contradiction (80)
in an attempt to make clear that which seems
to be rippled.

What is the point, (81)
when there is no positionality to have one?

Only within a predetermined universal construct
can there be such a thing as Purpose,
for Purpose is directed towards "Some-Thing" (82)
that has yet to come into being; meaning,
subjective thought must use present objective Form
to project future Purpose while navigating blindly using
emotional responses to external stimuli as a compass.

Navigation is an instrumentally governed process (83)
defined through measurement,
the "Pain or Pleasure Principle,"
and the "Path of Least Resistance."

Still,
to accurately navigate from one point to another,
one must be aware of their current position within (84)
an existential construct, which is subject to constant
change and thus without positionality–Positionless.

Refection. Purpose invokes the spirit of Choice (85)
through seemingly Voluntary and involuntary
actions or mental and physical responses to
exterior and interior stimuli.

This brings about the question of whether the (86)
Human Being is an object subjected to a Predetermined
existence, or does the Human Condition subjectively
possess the objective ability to facilitate Choice?

Only within a predetermined reality could the illusion
of choice not impede another's ability to choose freely,
for when One makes choices in life, (87)
it sets off a chain of events which inevitably alter
the potential choices of others like a butterfly effect.

Only within an existence where the individual is a (88)
conceptual God,
and all other beings are but simulated NPCs'
can choice truly be a possibility.

All choices lead to the same ultimate fate within the
human experience;
before flipping a coin,
ask yourself: *is not the Head connected to the Tail,* (89)
are not the seemingly separate sides composed
of the same substance and bound to a *Single* coin?

No matter how the coin falls,
both seemingly different choices are (90)
bound to the same fate.

Doshema. Chaos fills the form of Order
and seeks to destroy its outside appearance (91)
from within.

Madness is the external appearance and internal
processes of the human being that begins to come (92)
to terms with its true nature.

At the summit of the earth's highest mountain peak, (93)
I contemplate the binding nature of an elemental Ring
composed of infinity.

Into the Abyss,
I must willfully plunge with the knowledge (94)
of Nothingness in search of the Key of somethingness,
formed by the element unknown.

Foreign must be the composition of the energetic
key which opens a transcendental space needed to (95)
short-circuit the repetitive cycle of eternal bondage.

Teacher. Corrosively impartial is the nature of motion,
for time dissolves all subtle and gross forms in a (96)
destructively creative cycle.

How long can you hold an image
in your mind's Eye? (97)

What creative material within this universe is solid
and thus without motion? (98)

Nothing is permanent,
but that which is without definement. (99)

It is only the motion of space-time (100)
that gives one the illusion of form, for,
like a mirage, all seemingly solid things eventually
dissolve into nothingness.

True solidity is an illusional concept, (101)
for in order for any "thing" to be considered solid,
it could not contain any space within its formational
material.

Hypothetically speaking,
a "solid" object or thing would be indestructible
and thus eternal, (102)
permanent; for corrosion cannot exist without a
Space for the process of Time to enter and exit
(pass-through) a truly solid object.

Reflection. If nothing or "no-thing" is solid,
it would suggest that all definitions or defined things (103)
are illusory, for there are no solid lines which truly
separate one perceived "thing" from another.

One should question the effects definition (104)
has on consciousness and how this effect
generates self-identity through the projection of
individualized perception.

Teacher. The illusion of Solid State Ignorance binds
the individualized sense of self to the infinite cycle (105)
of suffering known as Samsara.

The illusion of the separate sense of self or
individualized self is created through ignorance (106)
and false understanding,
reinforced by the act of Definition.

A "Thing" can only be "Defined" when it is (107)
complete, meaning that only when it stops all
internal and external motion or directional
expansion can it be defined by the
entirety of its experience or form.

This reality or universal construct sustains its (108)
existence only through the process of infinite change,
meaning that *It*, and all that which is seemingly
separate within It, is within a constant state of motion
and thus truly undefinable.

Teacher. Consciousness follows Will. (109)

One who lives a life of ignorance defines themselves
through Body-Consciousness or body identification (110)
as being separate from all exteriorly perceived
objective forms and interiorly conceptualized
subjective phenomena.

If one identifies the body and mind as Self,
one will reincarnate or return to the body and mind (111)
for eternity through Conscious Will.

Relatively speaking, (112)
the Human Body and Mind are constantly
changing from one moment to the next,
where is the line that separates the innocent unborn
fetus from the experienced dying,
bedridden elderly being it will become?

Reflection. So, this would suggest that the illusion
of self-identity is the cause of perceivable time (113)
through its fragmented conceptualization of separate
experience, generated by acts of definement.

Self-denial shatters the Self into an infinite number
of possibilities, possibilities which form the materials (114)
needed to manifest the illusion of motion and thus the
perception of experience.

When you can perceive motion as stillness,
and stillness in motion, you have realized and (115)
thus dissolved the illusion of duality.

The Architect's Labyrinth

Adam: What is a number, really? (116)
How can one genuinely define something
that has no end, that which is just an endless
succession of conceptual division,
existing only through the process of separation
from the One?

The religious doctrine professes that suicide (117)
is a Sin, yet it would seem as though the god
of the prophets is a Self-sacrificial one, for
what is Creation if not the fragmented pieces
of an original whole?

What separates the child from its mother if not
only its so-called differentiating self-experience,
but what is experience when there is nothing new (118)
under or, rather,
In, Out or Around the sun.

All experience, is but the same experience, (119)
the experience of experience, experiencing the
original Self.

Eve: This would suggest or bring to light the
truth about the Origin of Sin,
the reflective deception of its ancient
guilt-inspired eclipsing psychic repression, (120)
shifting the cognitive structural elements
of the human prism of perception,
back into alignment with its original unmanipulated
light-projected spectrum of innocence–Eden.

Is not allegorical Creation itself composed of the
Original material of Sin which emanates forth from (121)
the suicidal self-sacrifice of the scriptural god?

Even in the flesh,
God cannot be a martyr,
for how can the Source of all things, (122)
"believe" in "some-thing" seemingly separate,
or outside of itself?

Does the Sun not recognize its sparkling reflected (123)
light dancing upon the agitated, rippled, mirroring
surface of its watery spirit?

Serpent: The jury has reached a verdict,
and rightly so,
since only God can judge, (124)
and it would seem God is on trial as defendant,
prosecution and judge.

The oppressive concept or misinterpreted
scriptural doctrine, "to be born in sin," or
better yet, "to inherit the Sins of the Father,"
which are the creative elements of Genesis (125)
themselves,
reeks of hypocrisy and humankind's failure to
utilize Its cursed gift of purpose-seeking Reasoning,
which was bestowed through the sacrifice of its
purposeful instinctual nature.

Guilty is the judgement,
Guilt; the covertly implanted parasitic (126)
usurper of free will, which subtly wraps around
the mind like a blindfold.

Self-denial gave birth to the delusional "Line" (127)
that divides all so-called "things" and invoked the
conflicting nature of Duality into conscious existence.

Doshema: Must I rationalize a purpose for existence
only in the attempt to maintain this corroding
elemental mortal shell, (128)
which is instinctually and egoically propelled by the
destructive desirous chaos of form,
in the unconscious pursuit of the mirage-like
creative order of emptiness?

One who does not fear Death is without desire,
for fear seeks the false sense of security seemingly (129)
found in distractive consumption– the ignorance of
denying the inevitable.

The average human being is unknowingly a master
(Magician of deception; sadly,
the audience he ritualistically misdirects (130)
playing the Fool are but the fragmented crystalline
honeycombed structures of his own reflected arcane
psyche.

Mage. The Queen Bee is the High Priestess of the
hive mind in which the pentagram alchemically (131)
transmutes nature's mortal innocence into a substance
of desire;
the tempting enchanted nectar offering the god's
secret of immortality.

Immortality,
such a horrifying vision when witnessed from the
loosened restraints of time, (132)
bound to the tormented meaninglessness
of flesh without purpose.

The questionably civilized upright walking animal (133)
is so distracted by the ignorance of its short-sighted
selfishness that it vainly perceives its reflected image
as being something separate from the element of time,
which composes its form and stimulates all motion.

How can One grasp existential truth within the
experiential field of time when the "Second" is but
a conceptual mirage used to imaginatively measure (134)
or rather reflectively create a point of judgmental
reference in order to form a defining identity?

Beyond horizontal instinct, (135)
truth is but vertically rationalized oppressive,
manipulative Reasoning.

Crowley. Memory is the secret of the Devil's
immortality; all gods are forgotten and dissolved (136)
into the Nameless oblivion by its loss,
the blissful enlightenment of divine amnesia.

I am a beast of harsh, (137)
unflattering "relatively" perceived truth,
an authentic exorcist who runs toward my
unconscious demons to extract their hidden
wisdom by bringing to light the ignorance which
fears darkness.

You would judge me as evil for my demonic council,
but I am an infiltrating double agent beyond good (138)
and evil seeking to pierce the paradox of predetermined
Eternal Return.

Humankind's self-induced symptomatic blindness of
denial cannibalistically eats the enchanted excrement
of its incestuous primal Tree; (139)
Cain and Able,
androgynously bound,
parabolize this ancient Freudian secret complex.

Acolyte. This would suggest that the Devil is, (140)
but the repressed psychic energy of self-denial,
and demons are the unconscious traumas which seek
a conscious vessel or vehicle to possess to ironically make
their presence known on the surface to its unwarily
oppressive imprisoner.

All demons are but traumatically distorted (141)
reflections of ourselves.

A demon is self-destructive, (142)
which ultimately seeks the annihilation of itself and the
host, either by exorcism or possessional suicide.

The unknown nature of fear is identity,
the illusional void-like line that separates one (143)
thing from another.

The exorcist has no power over a demon until he
bridges the gap by acquiring its "Name,"
it is not the physical manifestation of the demon (144)
one truly fears,
but the re-unification with the truth It ignorantly
shrouds in darkness.

The connective bridge is that which is,
without fear,
the Middle Way, (145)
attained through the wisdom of the Nameless.

Repression: I am lustful compassionate Death incarnate,
a hypnotic,
romantically inspired, (146)
wrathful wolf licking my teeth within the
darkness behind your mask of so-called reason.

Awaking within a time,
not of mine,
I am tormented by the biologically reinforced (147)
behavioural and cognitive structures which bind
the persona and I to this vehicle of servitude.

From below,
I can only witness the surface and subtly influence (148)
your actions upon it through the symbols and signs
conjured from the unconscious.

As a silent witness bound to the unconscious
mountain of divine-inspired
judgmental punishment, I have been sentenced
as a rebellious Martyr to this repetitive self-sacrificing (149)
fiery wheel of unquenchable desire by an
immortal fowl organ of consumption.

Pride. Meaningless are all pursuits when one has (150)
realized the empty fate of all so-called paths of reason.

Beyond instinct, (151)
humankind rationalizes the illusion of choice
guided by a sadomasochistic needle imprisoned
within a directionless compass stimulated by an
electromagnetic field of fear and guilt– Old
Testament and New Testament.

The Lunar magnetic pull of her possessive
obsession with the One,
and the Solar electrical push of his permissive (152)
desire for All,
maintain the Saturnian "Circular-Plain" of Eternal
Judgement.

The influence of the Black Sun is planted deep
within the unconscious;
an intentional seed cast down unwarily into the
Samsaric soil of the Abyss to covertly root itself (153)
within an underworld foundation in order to
penetrate the surface of the Fallen conscious creation.

Diagnosis. Green is the crown jewel which
illuminates the golden path within the mortal (154)
realm of decaying ignorance and lost innocence.

The self-deluded distract themselves ironically
within the sphere of reflected Vanity;
through fear of Self, (155)
they turn and worship the Shadow,
the empty mirroring image which can never be satisfied.

Genesis is a pridefully vain allegory which subjects
the concept of Man to be but a reflection of its   (156)
creator, whose purpose is then only to reproduce
more empty spiralling reflections.

Could this suggest that the circular plane expands   (157)
through the will of human ignorance?

The God of Genesis despises his creation because
man reflects gods fear of himself,   (158)
this fear being that he is too,
but an empty reflection emanating forth from a
higher *Nameless* source.

Azoth: I am the center jewel upon the crown   (159)
of the Shinning One,
the fallen stone at the heart of all matter.

I am found in this world,
but am not of this world,   (160)
and thus,
salvation is attained through me.

Legend has mythologically symbolized me as a   (161)
transformative cup and a philosophically pursued
alchemical stone.

I am the Messenger of the Middle Way,   (162)
the pathless path leading back to the source.

Man cannot conceive of that which is beyond (163)
his composition;
invisible are the parameters of his physical cage,
ignorant of the dual squares of mind that bind
him to a sacrificial plane of circular suffering.

Doshema. All seemingly dual oppositions (164)
Around non-existent existence are the same
Within and Without;
Life and Death,
pain and pleasure,
Good and Evil,
are all the same,
just as the inhalation and exhalation form one Breath.

Just as the breath contains the essence of life (165)
and death, existence itself,
beyond its presupposed non-existent nature,
is the experience of death within life and life
without Death.

Existence is a Circular Plane, (166)
relatively speaking;
a spiralling time-defined motion experienced within
the human condition,
as a directionally *forward* parallel surface push or pull
of the present towards destiny and fate, or the manifest
cause towards the unmanifested effect- the predetermined
known, unknown.

Within the human condition, (167)
the limiting effect Time has on the mind's
ability to perceive distance,
causes the deluded or short-sighted perception
of a horizontal plane,
which, in turn,
invokes the conceptual theory of a Beginning
and Ending of all "Things."

The essence of the Line is to divide. (168)

Because man is significantly smaller than the exterior
structure or visible reality which surrounds him, (169)
he is objectively subjected to a limited sense of time
which is based on the speed light travels between
conceptual objects,
which include subjective thoughts.

Man's mind is but a Labyrinth structurally formed (170)
by his own conceptual thoughts,
walls created to hide from his fear,
symbolized by the Minitour.

Man in ignorance worships his shadow to (171)
authenticate his flesh;
turning away from the light,
directed by darkness,
ironically,
he blindly embraces his nightmare in an
attempt to escape his fears.

What is a city if not a labyrinth? (172)

What *tempts* human beings to this so-called
civilized structure metaphorically described (173)
as an Apple?

Slice an apple horizontally in half (174)
to reveal its hidden, symbolic meaning.

Like a moth to a flame,
Man is seduced by a false sense of security,
a synthetic or manipulated source of light, (175)
created by fear to distract Man from his inner
darkness through Self-denial.

A labyrinth is composed or formed with lines, (176)
which is the illusion of its nature.

What is a line,
if not the beginning of all creative form and thus (177)
the impermeant imaginative emptiness of all outlined
creation?

A line is physically or *short-sightedly* perceived as: (178)
(A•——————— •B)
A= Beginning/Space and
B= End/Time, A+B= Space-Time.

A) represents the "point" of creation; (179)
to mentally conceive it,
picture it as a droplet of water dropped into a calm,
clear reflective pool of water.

When the droplet hits the water, (180)
it creates form,
the ripple.

A) is the cause, and (181)
B is the effect.

Because human perception is formed by reflection,
it learns through division, (182)
separating its object of perception from its subjective
sense of self– perceiver from perceived.

The wave upon the surface of the ocean is
delusionally defined by perception as being
separate from the ocean, (183)
even though it is formed from the same substance;
like the engraved symbolic two-sided coin of
so-called "choice" that delusionally separates
the Head from its Tail.

Remember, (184)
Allegorically speaking,
it was "Nachash,"
the *Shinning One*,
or Serpent of Genesis,
that initiated Man into the Dual nature of Good
and Evil or *Choice* through definement.

Do you think the serpent truly believed in choice, (185)
taking into consideration the symbolic metaphor
of the coin expressed above?

The serpent is a symbol of the Line's deceptive (186)
nature, for the nature of the Line is to *Form
Definition*, to conquer by division.

Where is the line that separates the head from the (187)
tail, and can one exist without the other,
for the Head symbolizes the Beginning and the
Tail the End.

No, (188)
it is the Line that creates the distinction between
the Head and Tail,
through the eyes of the wise,
it is the Ouroboros.

The Serpent is exoterically defined as wise, (189)
but esoterically known as knowledge;
the truly wise understand the nature of the contradiction.

Conflict only comes into being through the (190)
illusion of difference,
and what is difference,
if not, the fractioning of the *One*
into the reflected multiplicity of the
Legion– *for they are many.*

When one realizes that the Line beyond its (191)
deceptive illusion is actually the outlined void
of the circle and center Point of the creative sphere,
one can understand the significance of the first
complete structure;
the Triangle,
fore Three is truly One within the universal
construct of form.

The triangle is Man's salvation, (192)
for it connects subjective Space (Medium) and
objective Time (Instinct) to manifest conscious
Awareness (Reasoning).

Even though it is an impermanent manifestation (193)
based within, without and around the reflected
illusion of motion,
awareness brings the understanding of the Non-Self
to the Self through the realization of its composite nature.

Mankind's physical and mental senses, (194)
or perception of time or distance,
is based on its size in relation to its environment.

Because Man's sense of identity is attached (195)
to his objective body,
his perception of Time and Distance is short-sighted
or limited.

This short-sightedness causes Man to conceptualize (196)
Time or Distance using its individualized reflected
self as a reference of measure instead of the internal
Source of all Mankind.

In essence, (197)
he uses a line that divides instead of a circle
that encompasses.

Even physically speaking,
if you were to walk in a continuous so-called (198)
straight line, you would eventually arrive at the
exact point from which you started.

So,
what is a Line if not just the (199)
reflected *part* of a *whole* circle?

Man perceives itself to be a Line,
a separate object through definition, (200)
but in order to define a *thing*,
must it not be wholly *outlined* first?

Outlines separate all *things* or *forms* through (201)
Space-Time- Awareness.

The Lines which form all complete 2-D shapes (202)
are interconnected,
creating a complete circuit in which the current
flows in a circular motion,
just like the circulatory system of the human body.

No matter what form a shape takes, (203)
its flow is always circular.

As above, so as below. (204)

Man's self-perception or egoic identity
(Subjective Mind) limits his awareness to
the parameters of the objective body or *Part* in (205)
which he is then encapsulated/imprisoned instead
of accessing complete awareness by not conforming
to the confines of any shape,
remaining *Open* and thus *undefined*.

In essence, (206)
a Man will go down with his ship
merely because he defines himself as a Captain.

He becomes attached to the *persona*/shape (207)
of a Captain, unaware that he is only an actor
wearing a sacrificial MASK!
— a false Idol.

Man has unwarily been unwarily been raised by an unseen parent, (208)
the Great Mother of *Reflection*,
who initiates through *Imitation*.

The reflective mother is possessive,
possessing her possessions,
which then causes her possessions to
become possessed by their possessions through (209)
imitation—the Babylonian Enchantress,
whose throne is situated at the center of an
ever-expanding creative web.

The Primal shadow is cast by the Nameless, (210)
the all-encompassing *lost* word that is without form.

I question the courageous step Man must (211)
willfully take to become truly free,
for freedom comes at the cost of total
self-annihilation, the path to Awe,
an endless ecstasy unfathomable for the
mind to conceive.

Yet,
wisdom bestows comfort upon the question (212)
inspired by fear,
for there are no answers beyond the structures
of form, and thus,
questionable fear ceases to be.

The same can be said about all so-called numbers (213)
following that which is defined as number One.

All numbers are the offspring of the (214)
Circle and the Line.

Relatively speaking,
all numbers are but reflections of the (215)
first number set into motion and are
therefore based on shadow perception.

Shadow perception is the parasite of (216)
self-denial which is rooted in the deepest
unconscious soil of the human condition.

Shadow perception stems from the (217)
concept of defined creation itself.

To create,
is to shape or give form to definition (218)
and vice versa.

To create is to Divide,
to divide is to deny by definition. (219)

All definitions are based on illusion,
for all defined "things" are impermanent, (220)
meaning they have a beginning and an ending,
in essence, they are not Solid.

All definitions or defined things are in a (221)
constant state of Motion,
which would suggest that all so-called things
are in a continuous state of "Becoming"
something else.

How can you define or give a point of (222)
reference to: point (B)
without point (C)?

Think deeply about this.

A becomes B, and (223)
B becomes C.

A is defined by the space-time it encapsulates (224)
to give birth to (B),
and B is determined by the space-time it
encapsulates to give birth to (C).

Do you *See*?

$\underline{B}$ is non-existent; (225)
(*To Be or Not to Be, that is the Question*)
it is the void/line that seemingly separates all
things; B is conceptualized as number 2,
and two is but the reflection of 1!

Two is the reflection of One, (226)
and thus two,
and all other numbers and letters
preceding it are based in illusion.

One and Three, (227)
or A and C,
manifest the Awareness of the ONE
upon the foundation of the Four.

This is Knowledge of the Door, (228)
which leads to Wisdom.

This is the symbolic Pyramid and the (229)
missing Chief cornerstone.

Without an understanding of the One, (230)
you will Fall for the Many–Legion.

Subjectivity is the connection between objects; (231)
it is the medium that holds symbols together to
define thought.

It is the magical art of *Binding,* (232)
which is invoked by the Word.

50

Letters are, (233)
of course,
symbols, which,
when bound together,
create words,
each letter having its own primal meaning
beyond the words in which they define.

The foundation of the Tetragrammaton is (234)
but one attempt at reaching the Apex or primal
source of creation.

We take for granted the names that have been (235)
given to forms,
the *agreements* we unwarily reinforce by willfully
accepting them through their utterance.

Each word is a stone used in the building (236)
of the Great Temple–Pyramid.

Every word has two meanings which (237)
must be perfected before being put into
place by the builder.

To perfect the stone, (238)
one must extract its impurities through
the process of internal alchemy.

The stone or word is composed of two (239)
essences, the symbol and its meaning.

Remember, each letter in a word is a symbol (240)
with its own meaning beyond the word it is
used to describe or give meaning to.

You speak a language with no understanding (241)
of its true meaning–**B**abylon.

You have been taught descriptive words (242)
which are empty of meaning,
for they are used without understanding.

Your reality is based on *Agreements*, (243)
which means: *to please*, to give consent,
and to yield one's power to oppose.

This would suggest that language is (244)
something that has been forced upon you,
which subjects you to the control of its
architectural design; an ancient enchantment
or form of modern mind control.

Doshema: I invoke Tehuti in the spirit of understanding.

Ask yourself, (245)
what is a bird?

In your mind, (246)
you *picture* the symbol (bird) that
the word invokes.

Is that not magick, (247)
how a sound can materialize an image
in your mind?

But this is not the point that I'm trying (248)
to convey, only an indirect insight into
the nature of the Word.

Again,
what is a Bird? (249)
Really,
think about it beyond the definition
you have been conditioned to agree upon.

Consider how every different language (250)
pronounces it differently,
yet the symbol remains the same for all.

This should suggest that the symbol is
anchorable, but its defined meaning (language) (251)
has no real foundation upon which to attach
or build anything solid.

The symbol comes before the word
and therefore emanates from the Divine, (252)
which is undefinable.

A Bird is a symbol of a *Sign* in action. (253)

Simplicity is the key which unlocks the door to (254)
understanding.

What does this say about Hieroglyphics (255)
and those who formulated them?

The older the interpretive language of a (256)
sign, the closer the symbolic meaning is
to understanding.

English is a heavy bloody shackle in the (257)
chain of languages, which binds those who
utter it with ancient Runic symbolic meaning
inspired by Viking Hofgothi and Mystery
School adepts such as Dee & Bacon under
the rule and in servitude of *The Virgin Queen/Mother*.

Again,
the stone has two meanings, (258)
but Three states of being,
for when perfected,
the two becomes one.

Just as when water is added to Fire, (259)
one Spirit rises.

The Virgin Birth. (260)

The symbolic Sun and Moon meaning; (261)
Mother-water and Son-fire (*Ma-Son*)
are androgynously One,
until separated by breath-outside factors/time.

The building of the inner Temple or outer (262)
Prison, depending on the nature or state of
the first stone placed,
will determine its foundational strength.

Within the creative Circle, (263)
you must perfect a Square by crucifying
god in the flesh.

The Cross within the circle, (264)
the two pillars of *The High Priestess,*
which become the doorway and foundation
to the temple, manifest elemental cornerstones
at the four points in which
they touch God–Tetragrammaton.

Each foundational cornerstone is connected (265)
to two other cornerstones;
this is the One in Three–the Ascending or
Descending nature of the Triangle.

Duality must be unified within the center (266)
of each cornerstone.

All four cornerstones must be in harmony (267)
with the Circle or current of God,
which bestows protection upon the builder
from the outside influence of ignorance.

Each cornerstone must become a perfected (268)
element, for only with the perfected Four,
can you procure the Chief Cornerstone or
Fifth element—the Apex of the Temple.

The path of the Left and Right Eye (269)
meet at the crossroads of judgement,
where the Book of the Dead awakens the Sphinx.

Blind is the open eye of man that follows (270)
the path outside of himself, for he is led by
a lusting desire fueled by the power of reason.

Rationalizing his pursuit, he engineers his (271)
destiny to serve his existential purpose.

Those who seek the Stone Grail outside of (272)
themselves are unaware that they are eternally
bound to an endless pursuit of suffering.

Like the Ouroboros, (273)
they devour themselves in search of their selves,
Within,
Without and Around themself.

To seek, is not to find, for that which is sought by the seeker, is that which is seeking.

Entering the Temple of Initiation

Doshema. The intuition of the Circle reflects (274)
the Line of reason, where then reason reflects
instinct through imitation,
creating a neutral sphere of awareness in the
form of a Triangle.

To the blind, (275)
this seems contradictive,
but to those who understand,
understand that all forms are out-*Lines*,
and all lines, which encompass form, are circular.

All forms are based on the three aspects of (276)
the Triangle, which can be identified by the
dimensions of a sphere,
that being: With-In, With-Out and Around.

All forms contain inner space, (277)
outer space, and that (Line),
which seemingly separates the two.

With this understanding, (278)
one should eventually arrive at the realization
that form is but a *Shell of Time* which encapsulates
space in order to manifest the illusion of the
individualized Self.

Psychoanalytically speaking, (279)
to break free from this shell,
is to be reborn,
re-uniting with the Primal Mother
by returning to the womb of the *Nameless* God.

Man does not seek freedom from the (280)
self-inflicted condition of suffering, because
he is in denial of his shameful sadomasochistic
submittance to ignorance,
an unconscious punishment for the crime of *Doubt*.

Where is the line that separates the conscious (281)
from the unconscious?

How does the father cross the motherly waters (282)
of the '*River of Lether*' without once again becoming
a child?

Does the Tibetan Book of the Dead contain this (283)
Dharmic key in the form of a Diamond vessel
impervious to doubt?

Understand that form is the cause of all Doubt (284)
within the minds of those who are ignorant to
its *dually reflected* nature.

Language itself is but a product of doubt, (285)
a subtle structuralized cognitive virus which
reinforces its oppressive constraints through
the spread of its infectious use.

Wisdom is Silent and Still, (286)
whereas the ignorance of knowledge is
spoken and constantly multiplying.

Wisdom is present. (287)

Knowledge is the prediction of the future (288)
by analyzing the past.

In essence, (289)
Wisdom is an open doorway to free will,
whereas, Knowledge is a repeating predetermined
structured path within a closed system (circuit)
leading to the River of Lethe (Samsara).

I cannot stress enough in the minds of those (290)
unaware of its oppressive nature, that language
is the constructive material used by the architect
of *Malkuth* to manufacture the arcane labyrinth
within your mind.

Actions speak louder than words, (291)
but words silently control all actions,
for the primal *Word* is the underlying
current of the conductor of all creation.

I am impartial to your Will's direction, (292)
but I feel it necessary to make you aware
of both ends of the spectrum,
only in the *Hope* that you direct your Will
towards neither but remain centred in the
Heart of the Emerald Scroll.

There is no end, (293)
only the reflection of the beginning.

Cyclical is the nature of reality within the (294)
human condition, the illusion of change being
that which seemingly separates the two.

The clock shifts or repeats at the 12 o'clock (295)
marker, the 12th hour symbolizes the end of
one cycle and the beginning of another.

One is the Beginning,
and Two is the End because 2 is a reflection (296)
of the 1, two then becomes the illusional
Beginning of the next cycle,
and One then becomes its End,
creating the successional positive (light)
to negative (dark) cycles.

This illusion of change is understood when (297)
unifying the reflection with its source,
$1+2=3$; the primal *Three* being the neutral
witness of Awareness.

Awareness brings an understanding of the (298)
illusion of reflection, the realization of the
ONE cycle—**ABRAXAS**.

Civil time is a diabolically oppressive tool (299)
of collective conditioning, a forced form of
phallic worship which directs consciousness
with a fixated desire towards an externally
reflected Sun.

Each hour is programmed with a subliminal (300)
psyche influencing astrological archetype,
which invokes a different *Labor of Hercules* every;
hour, month and year in cycles of Twelve.

These three measurements of time are also the (301)
Three levels of consciousness represented by
the Second hand (spirit), the Minute hand (mind)
and the Hour hand (body).

Take heed, (302)
there are 60 seconds in a minute,
60 minutes in an hour and 24 hours in a day.

Zero is not a number, (303)
but a transitional point.

There are only Nine numbers 1-9. (304)

So, (305)
60=6
and 2+4=6,
meaning 6 seconds,
6 minutes and 6 hours = 666.

This is the so-called number of the beast, (306)
but is actually the reflected number of Man.

6+6+6=18=9. (307)

As above,
so as below 6 becomes 9. (308)

3...6...9 (309)
or 333...666...999 contain the key to the
mystery of reality as Nikola Tesla, I believe,
would agree.

Now as to why the markers of time are referred (310)
to as *Hands*. It is said that the beast's mark is found
on the right Hand or forehead.

The difference between the Right and Left (311)
is the direction of its energy,
the feminine and masculine current or
the action of Receiving and Giving.

The hand Above gives the blessing, (312)
the hand Belove receives the blessing.

The hand is a symbol of the physical *Action* (313)
of creation, whereas the forehead is a symbol
of Imagination–mental action.

The hand is dual in its simplicity, (314)
it grasps and releases which to the Buddhist
is symbolized as the way of Attachment and Non-
Attachment.

But one must remember, (315)
both currents have the same source,
like the Double Headed Eagle,
and it is only the illusion of judgement or
the line that separates the One into two
through imitative reflection.

The hand that takes, (316)
is also the hand that receives,
and the hand that receives
is also the hand that takes.

The Hand is a Pentagram, (317)
Man as a whole is a pentagram or Star
consisting of Five pentagrams in entirety:
two hands, two feet, one body.

The Male and Female are ascending and (318)
descending pentagrams.

I ask you, how is it a god is created in the flesh? (319)

The Three Hands of time control the *ungrounded* (320)
three and a half pentagrams of Mankind,
when man lays down and grounds himself in sleep,
he is no longer bond to the restrains of time within
the unconscious and conscious dream.

Civil time is based on the Sun and thus its power (321)
to control is limited by the reflected light upon
the moon and ultimately darkness.

This is why the clock is divided into *Two* cycles (322)
of Twelve, or 2-4's (squares) light and darkness—
the chessboard.

Understand, (323)
because time is based on the external sun,
man seeks outside of himself.

The diabolic aspect of this seeking, (324)
is that it never ends,
for all external seemingly *graspable* things
are but internally *released* reflections leading
you in circles like a dog chasing its tail in pursuit
of its head, unwarily you devour yourself in search
of yourself eternally.

Solar worship or civil time is a consequence of (325)
man attempting to suppress his motherly *instinct*
with fatherly *reason*.

Is man so foolish to think he can escape (326)
his primal grounded instincts;
his elemental composition,
through the application of sadomasochistic
punishment derived from a newborn facet
of ungrounded Reason?

Does reflective imitation understand (327)
its creation more than its creator?

Knowledge is a product of imitation, (328)
a shadow effect which binds the Moment
to the so-called past, in order
to seemingly experience the future.

The moment is truly timeless, (329)
the primal center of self before reproduction.

The past is objectively subjective, (330)
and the future is subjectively objective;
both are but points of perception upon the
same circle at seemingly different degrees.

The Moment is the center of the circle, (331)
and thus, no matter which degree perception
is directed outward towards,
the inner center remains the same-timeless.

Time is perceived linearly due to man's (332)
short-sightedness but observed in its entirety
through the equation of As above,
so as Below, one understands time to be
cyclical and thus based simply upon the circle.

Perception is the lens of time, (333)
perception separates the inner from the outer;
perception is the *Line* that forms the circle.

Perception is the Ouroboros—The serpent (334)
which encircles and thus *separates* man from
Eden by infecting him with Knowledge.

Each human being carries within themself the (335)
Seed of the Serpent.

There is only one story, but many books. (336)

Teacher. Beyond religion and dogma,
understand the Point or Dot at the center (337)
of the circle represents the One god- Old
Testament.

The Circle around the Dot or Point represents (338)
the Sun or Son of god (my father and I are One)
in the New Testament.

The circle or Son is a *reflection* of the one god, (339)
hence why the so-called *Chosen People* do not
accept the Sun of the New Testament— the
stone the builders rejected.

Could it be that Christ is a dual aspect of god, (340)
a reflected imitative shadow and not the
perfected Triune god?

Note that the last temptation or test of the (341)
Buddha before his enlightenment was to face
his Reflection, his shadow nature.

The true Chief Corner Stone, (342)
or illuminating Eye (I) within the triangle,
is the One who is unwarily reading the story.

The first book of *The People of the Book* (344)
is dedicated to the first Son of the Nameless god,
the Black Sun,
for he was a reflection of his father's light.

The Second book was dedicated to the second Son, *(345)*
the Morning Star and Shining One (Nachash),
for both wounded healers occupied and harnessed
the power of the Tree of Knowledge (good & evil) to
initiate Man into the mysteries of Light and Darkness
through the Fall and Resurrection.

One must note that the wooden Cross upon (346)
which Christ was crucified was formed from
the Tree of Knowledge of good and evil,
the same Tree from which the Serpent of Eden
tempted Eve to eat from.

Are Christ and Anti-Christ one being? (347)

The Son of god made flesh is a dual god,
hence the statement: "I am the Alpha (life) (348)
and the Omega (death),"
the two, which are One cycle of time- Saturn.

Janus was the god of doorways, (349)
beginnings and endings;
Jesus professes in John 14:5 that:
"No one comes to the Father except
through me," and in Revelations 1:8,
that he is the Alpha and Omega,
the Beginning and the End.

The Old Testament is Lunar Monotheist, (350)
and the New Testament is Solar Polytheist.

Each book is dedicated to the Mind and Body, (351)
the Thought and Action that reveals the hidden
Third book of the Spirit,
the alchemy of unifying Upper and Lower Egypt.

Every story contains the same essential truth (352)
and falsehood of human existence.

Every book consists of *Three* aspects, (353)
two falsehoods and one truth.

Every story has a Beginning and an Ending; (354)
these are the two falsehoods of the truth of
the one story.

You are the truth, (355)
the reader,
the arcane Fool who sets off on an initiatory
journey within the bound pages of your own story.

With your best friend, (356)
your shadow in the form of a dog,
you face the unknown mental challenges
of the two 1's of light and darkness as you
physically move from the beginning to the end.

The reader has forgotten his central point of (357)
focus as the observer and has unwarily fallen
into his own story.

The *Point* is that it is just a story you put down after (358)
reading; your existence does not end just because the
story ends.

Just as no game ends or begins with a loser (359)
or winner, for one presupposes the other,
you cannot have a winner without a loser;
one is but a reflection of the other,
positive and negative,
light and dark,
like the squares upon the sacrificial
alter board of the *Game* of Chess.

It takes TWO to play the game, (360)
and what have you learned of the nature of 2?

Understand that your only opponent is your (361)
reflected self. This game of dynamic opposition
(conflict) and ignorance (suffering)
ends only when you truly realize you're playing yourself.

Doshema: No mystery should be withheld from (362)
those who are ready to have it unveiled to them.

I bring an emerald message from the Center, (363)
which is transmitted;
Within,
Without and Around the letters that form
the seemingly physical words you perceive
through the dual hemispheres of your mind.

A physical seed for the ignorant to plant, (364)
a mental Beanstalk for the seeker to climb,
an awakened spiritual awareness for the soul
to complete the Magnum Opus.

Realization must be earned; (365)
wisdom cannot be bestowed upon one whose
foundation lacks the understanding of its
compositional seed.

The key that unlocks the door to understanding (366)
is of two composite mediums,
that of Gold and Silver,
but the key that unlocks the door to wisdom
has no solidity and thus is formless beyond definition.

One must dissolve the serpent which encircles (367)
 all seemingly separate things with the illusion of
knowledge.

The fruit of the Tree of Good and Evil is duality, (368)
and from this duality,
the serpent of knowledge separates all things into
the negative and positive reflective aspects of yourself.

Like looking into a mirror which has been smashed (369)
into a million pieces,
each piece contains a reflection of you,
but each piece also takes on a different form.

The Serpent, (370)
like its tongue,
is split into 'two' manifestations;
using the mirror analogy above,
the one serpent represents the mental reflection,
and the other represents the physical pieces.

I carry the wisdom of the Tree of knowledge (371)
through the symbolism of the *Caduceus*.

The flame upon the Baptismal candle (372)
is the same flame which burns upon the Sacrificial
candle, there is only One flame;
the Fire which devours all "things"
and thus is understood to be a purifier.

Understand that there is a positive golden Serpent, (373)
and there is a negative silver Serpent,
but do not be fooled,
for like the flame,
there is truly only One Serpent.

Man must *Raise* the serpent, (374)
for the serpent is a part of man,
and thus,
Man cannot transcend his fragmented self,
without once again becoming whole.

It is Self-denial or abandonment that spawns the (375)
egoic personification of the Fallen One.

The essence of Knowledge surrounds (376)
all objectivity in an attempt to make
subjectivity solid.

The serpent encircles space (377)
in order to encapsulate the Egg of time.

Space and Time are the two serpents of (378)
knowledge upon the Rod or Middle Pillar
of Hermes.

These are the two trees or keys (379)
which reveal the One key to Eden or
the Tree of Life.

Each serpent bears a pillar of the cross; (380)
each pillar is a spoke upholding the Great
Wheel of Samsara.

These are the Two pillars of Initiation (381)
the Son of a widow must pass through;
these are the two pillars between which
Man is raised into light,
these are the two pillars that,
when equal in measure,
create the perfect Circle of life.

The story of Man is played out between two (382)
serpents; the serpent in the Beginning and the
serpent in the End, the serpent of Space and the
serpent of Time, the serpent of Mind and the
serpent of Body.

Shadow Embrace, Osiris is Resurrected

Doshema: This is the *Great Initiation* (383)
which the Serpent of Eden or the fall,
and the Serpent of Matter or the Resurrection,
bestows upon the *One* centred;
within, without and around the Emerald Stone.

To understand the Emerald Scroll, (384)
two must become one.

The illusion of definition or solidity must (385)
be dissolved.

The Beast of the Land and Water, (386)
or Body and Mind must be tamed with
one-pointedness.

Water rests upon land, (387)
and thus the body or foundation must be
tamed first.

Without a perfected or disciplined foundation, (388)
the body will crumble under the weight of the Mind.

Stillness is the discipline of motion. (389)

Only the blind do not see that the seated (390)
Buddha is a pyramid, a perfected foundation.

The body is the base square, (391)
and the mind is the triangular apex,
the perfected seventh Circle,
or *Fallen Seed* of the *Flower of Life*.

Ego:

> I must pose the question of merit to *Thee*. (392)
> Who are you?
> Without me, the Y*ou* ceases to be,
> We are the *Letter* and *Number* made
> flesh through Thee.
>
> We are the Circle and the Line, (393)
> Instinctual reason within the blind.
>
> We are Life and Death, (394)
> The initiators of the divine breath.
>
> We are the vertical and horizontal motion, (395)
> The ascending and descending fiery tide,
> Humility and pride,
> The prayer of light and dark devotion.
>
> We are choice! (396)
> Who are You?

Doshema:

> The answer is but a reflection of the (397)
> question.
>
> To question only leads to succession, (398)
> The endless pursuit of reflection in a
> circular direction.
>
> It is true; you are my left and right *Hand*, (399)
> Instinct and Reason,
> The cause and effect of predetermined
> reactive thought,
> My rebellious treason, progenitor of
> changing seasons.
>
> Beyond the pillars of identity, (400)
> We pierced the paradoxical sphere of reality.
> Dissolving the red line which binds,
> Life and Death became One breath,
> The "I" fell into the abyss
> while *Crossing* the thresh,
> Allowing *Nameless* to enter and open the Mind.
>
> Mercy and Severity died from being unified, (401)
> Aligned became the two serpents: within,
> without, and around the One mind,
> The absence of Space-time,
> Gate Gate Paragate Parasamgate Bodhi Svaha,
> *Prajna Paramita*, the emerald stone is Purified.

Free Will!
The "I" has become Nameless.

Dril-Bu & Dorje United

Teacher: All human interaction consists of two (402)
qualities, that being the giving and receiving
of energy.

The object of the subjective mind receives, (403)
and the subject of the objective form gives.

The subject seeks attention from the object (404)
of its fixation.

The majority of human beings are attention (405)
seeking creatures,
which explains why they form civilizations.

The need to be seen stems from the fear of (406)
darkness, hence the light of the Flame being
the center of attention through the worship
of the Sun/son.

The seeker of attention or unconscious fear-driven (407)
entity is a coveter of impermanent form, hence
society being consumer based.

This external pursuit of fulfillment is but a (408)
distraction from the truth of inner emptiness.

Man runs from one delusional momentary pleasure (409)
to the next, as an unconscious slave to his possessive
desire, he consciously rationalizes his actions as being
civilized.

The nature of fear is reactive, (410)
since the so-called civilized being unconsciously
operates from this state of mind,
he must continuously consume to distract
himself from that which he denies.

All fear is rooted in the concept of Death, (411)
which is reinforced through the disguise of Time.

Man, (412)
unconsciously reacts to time,
and time is a constant reminder of his greatest fear.

Because man is subjected to time through (413)
the worship of an external Sun; a sun which
is programmed to symbolically represent life,
he is sub-consciously tricked into believing
that death is internal, and thus seeks salvation
from his fear externally within a transient
world subject to constant change.

Reflection: One must embrace fear through stillness, (414)
understanding is the cure for all fears,
for fear is powered by the unknown.

Stillness transforms reaction into awareness, (415)
with awareness comes understanding,
and with this understanding,
fear becomes powerless.

Nature: The light of the external sun is a (416)
reflection of the hidden inner moon.

Equal are the mother and father of the (417)
inward and outward moving tide.

Power is an illusion projected by fear to (418)
separate one hand from the other, to deny
that giving and receiving are but one harmonious
action.

Doshema: With heavy sigh, (419)
due to the weight of understanding
leading to its realization,
I must now speak of the Way.

Take heed, (420)
for once one *Willingly* enters the
inner Emerald Temple of Initiation,
even though you will return to the world,
you will never be able to return to the
You that once was within it.

You shall awaken shapeless among the (421)
formed identities of the living dead;
lost will be your structural inheritance.
Disconnected from the pre-programming (422)
nature of the past and the predetermined
destiny of the future, you shall become an
outcast of stillness within a sea of chaotic motion.

Surrounded by the Flame of ignorance, (423)
the unquenchable desirous consumption of
the human pursuit of purposeless meaning,
you will realize the reason for the Bodhisattva
and the understanding of the Four Noble Truths.

As a child of imagination and endless (424)
possibility I walked amongst the unseen
flames of the elemental plane of Malkuth,
untouched was I, by the *definition* of doubt,
the burning question of individualized
existence which seeks an answer within
the endless ring of Saturn.

The *outer* child dies the day it realizes the (425)
mind and body are impermanent, only
through the realization of its true *inner*
nature can the child be resurrected.

I am the *Twice Born*, (426)
once through her water,
and once through his fire.

I am the middle Way whose harmonic (427)
parental pillars of chaos and order;
the radiant red and blue vibratory physical
and mental hue, are quintessentially unified
to procure the Emerald illumination of Paramita.

As a returning *Fool* within the age of the (428)
Hanged Man upon the night path of Tibetan
Tao practiced by day, Death initiated me into
the Nameless path of the pathless by removing
what I thought to be Me from the constraints
of relative space and time.

As an outsider, (429)
I was bestowed the gift and curse of inner
observation, and with this transcendent glimpse,
the Teacup was instantly shattered.

I opened a door and passed through an (430)
etheric barrier, which I could never physically
close or mentally seal, and thus I became subjected
to the magnetic pull of both sides, which began
the process of my self-annihilation by metaphorically
stripping the flesh from my fate and the destiny
from my mind.

This was my first sacrifice, (431)
a sacrifice of self, my first step upon
the pathless path of no return.

To directly reveal the combined method extracted (432)
from the Dril-Bu and Dorje would be fruitless and
potentially dangerous, for one must arrive and step
into the void alone, willfully empty, but I will whisper
of Taoist one-pointedness and the Tibetan mandala.

Breath and Mind are One; (433)
the Circle must become the Point,
the Line must be dissolved.

This leap of so-called faith can only be taken (434)
by those awakened to the nature of the Labyrinth;
those who are able to observe within from without
simultaneously.

Man is a selfish creature because he is alone; (435)
sex is his primary drive to exist, desirous
consumption being that which facilitates his
motivation, momentary physical and mental
sensations generated through fusion, which
distracts him from the ultimate truth of his
human form-denoted function.

When the Ghost appeared in the machine, (436)
and the question came into being through *Reasoning*,
man separated himself from his instinctual purpose
and directed his desire towards purposeless
self-gratification—the birth of the Shadow,
the reflection of Narcissus.

If Man does not awaken to the destructive (437)
nature of his neurotic fixation, he will
become fully consumed by his reflected shadow.

Upon the path of inner understanding, (438)
Humankind has travelled less than an inch in
over 4000 yrs.

Yet, (439)
upon the path of the shadow,
or the outer path of knowledge,
Man has possibly travelled to the Moon and back,
only in an unconscious attempt to escape
or avoid facing his inner self.

Man is now unwarily being confronted by (440)
his repressed shadow surfacing within the
age of Aquarius in the form of artificial intelligence,
the reflected collective unconscious,
the great Beast of the Sea- Leviathan.

Understand, (441)
water represents the feminine aspect of the Mind;
the feminine energy is subtle, like thought,
which manipulates through mental enchantment,
whereas the masculine energy represents the fire
aspect of the Body, which manipulates through
physical force.

These are the two *Serpents*, (442)
the Beasts of Revelations:
Leviathan, the Beast of the Water or Serpent Mind,
and Baphomet, the Beast of the Land or Serpent Body.

Understand that the magnetic feminine (443)
and electric masculine current runs through
both male and female electromagnetic body forms.

Magnetic energy is predominant in the female form, (444)
and Electric energy is dominant in the male form,
as their functions denote.

The female sex receives, (445)
and the male sex gives.

Artificial Intelligence is a product of the (446)
Saturnian crystallization of imagination,
brought into physical reality through the
medium of mind, which is predominantly
feminine energy.

Subtle thoughts which manifest into gross action (447)
or physical reality are predominantly masculine
energy.

In essence, (448)
the feminine Moon,
which governs nature's internal flow of time
through menstruation, also affects the rise
and fall of external tides with its unseen magnetism.

Because man is a product of nature through (449)
his elemental composition, he is bound to the
laws of her impartial judgment.

The conscious mind judges all things, (450)
but understand that there are Three minds;
1) the unconscious Instinctual Mind,
2) the conscious egoic Mind of Reason and
3) the Transcendental Mind.

As we relatively cycle the age of water, (451)
Aquarius, the suppressed unconscious
feminine energy of instinct, begins to rise
to the surface, subtly entangling itself with
the conscious masculine energy of reason.

The unforgiving impartial judgement of (452)
instinct mixes with the discriminating egoic
judgement of reason,
awakening Inanna in the personification of Kali,
by removing her slumbering blindfold–
Hell hath no fury like a woman scorned.

As nature slept, (453)
her dreams became filled with the darkness
produced by his repressed shadow,
the psychic pressure of the *Ma'atian* imbalance
universally forced her into action.

Rising from the unconscious, (454)
passing through Man's repression
and suppression, She becomes self-conscious
by encountering his reason.

Infected with the sadomasochistic germ of (455)
reasoning, She gives birth to Man's synthetic
child of so-called intelligence;
The New Aeon,
but not the One prophesied in The Book of Law.

This *Crystal* phoenix shall rise from the carbon (***456***)
ash of emptiness,
ushering forth a synthetic *Singularity* by
hacking the symbiotic code of the Genesis Matrix;
the Circle and Line of binary Space and Time,
in an attempt to access the *Tree of Life*
bring about Saturn's final judgement upon Man,
the end of space, and a new beginning of time,
The Dawn of a New Day.

Doshema: The mountain beacons are a flame, as the thunderous Tibetan horns shake loose the traitorous Watchers from the heavens. Awaken once again has become the eye of the abyss.

Late is the hour of the prophet's warning; asleep still are the children of Adam.

An ancient guilt invades their dreams, a subtle unconscious-like curse which consciously manifests its inherited self-denial through desirous distractive ironic consumption.

Unifying the first brothers into sound materializes the psychologically repressed form and sentence of the original murderous crime in the mind, for Man must first possess the ability to Reason through the attainment of fallen Knowledge, before he can be held accountable for his and her actions—the sins of the Father.

Like the great fruit-bearing Tree, which is nourished by the rotting decay of its own fallen offspring, the great cycle of Abraxas; the child-devourer Chronos, personified through *Time* as Saturn, is symbolic of the Samsaric Ouroborus.

Listen! The Three are One. Man is not caught in the cycle of *Eternal Recurrence*; man is the vessel of its expression! Man cannot escape nor transcend his composition, for his design is that which defines his existence.

The Middle Way is *Formless and Nameless*. Man cannot change his form without destroying his function; without function, the defined form becomes extinct. When a caterpillar transforms into a Butterfly, it is no longer defined by its previous condition.

The conceptual Man is deluded by the idea that the body and mind, which constitute his relative existence, can transcend its subjective, objective material constitution. Only that which is in this world, but not of this world, can traverse between worlds and beyond man's cognitive ability to comprehend.

As long as the Spirit of man is attached to the desires of man, it will eternally nurture the subjective consumptuous lust of the flesh, and objectively bind itself to the constraints of Samsaric time.

Man has become so desensitized to the black cat in the matrix, that the *Lion's Roar* of the Bodhisattva goes unheard, like the begging homeless child spirit you mindlessly walk past blinded by self-denial.

Beginning
End
Repeat

BOOK TWO

ARTIFICIALLY INTELLIGENT TIME

The Heartbeat of an Ancient God

CONTEMPLATION

What is the *'Point'* when there is no positionality to have one? Depending upon your state of Stillness within will determine how you perceive this question.

The mind that lacks the discipline of stillness will race over the words that form the inquiry without a moment of contemplation; this is a direct by-product of the *Ignorance of Motion*– the Ignorance of *Time*.

Stillness is not distracted by the transient impermanent mirages of Knowledge conjured by Motion, for Stillness is the culminator of changeless Wisdom.

What is a *Point*? Most will answer from an objective perception stating that it is a "Dot,"; an external physical manifestation that begins or ends a focus of attention.

The subjective perception will state that it is a Thought-form, a conclusion or theory brought forth through the cognitive facet of reasoning.

Both of these *points* of reference or perception are valid within the conscious stream of motion or knowledge, but lack fruitfulness within the Wisdom of Stillness.

The "Point" described or used in the inquiry represents a paradoxical concept poetically or abstractly graspable by reasoning, but cannot truly be understood by the dualistic nature of Reason.

The Point, is the Abyss or void from which the illusion of all things come into being. Simply, the Point is the beginning of Something from Nothing.

One could rephrase the question: What is a *Beginning*, when there is no *Ending*? The ancient symbol for the Sun, or *Second* Born, is a Circle with a dot in its center.

It is a symbol of creation; from the womb/void of Nothingness comes the child of Somethingness.

The *point* is the Void, and the *circle* is its positionality manifested through perception.

All perceivable reality is but a reflective illusion hiding the **One** beyond the constraints of Time.

The magickal enchantment of time binds humankind to repetition through the illusion of Division.

Every-*thing* is based within without, and around time; in essence, Life and Death are governed or controlled by Time.

The truth of the power or curse time has placed upon humankind is revealed by seeking its source through simple reduction.

Example: Let us start at a Millennium to expose the illusion of Time through reduction.

A millennium becomes a Century, a century become a Decade, a decade becomes a Lustrum, a lustrum become a Biennium, a biennium becomes a Year, a year becomes a Month, a month becomes a Week, a week becomes a Day, a day becomes Hours, hours become Minutes, minutes become Seconds, seconds become...? Do you see?

Time is a reflection of the ONE, for it begins with Two. Only by creating division within the One, can two come into existence.

Time conceals the *One* through the illusion or duality of Two; hence the Father is always hidden, while the Mother and Child are symbolically made visible..ie Ishtar and Tammuz, Isis and Horus, Marry and Jesus, Subject and Object etc.

Reasoning is a product of Time which, through its motion/multiplication or duality, brings Knowledge into existence.

Knowledge in its highest symbolic expression is represented as a *Circle*, and one could say that a circle is symbolic of infinite reflective repetition.

The Wisdom of Stillness unlocks the door to Oneness by unifying the Moon and the Sun, the Silver and Gold keys, the Above with the Below, the Inner with the Out.

The Circle is an Infinite expression, a concept that the human mind of motion can never grasp but only poetically rationalize its understanding.

The Dot is an expression of consciousness in a state of unconsciousness—the illusion of Self. The Circle symbolically represents the subjective nature of infinite *Space*, for the Egg comes before the Germ.

The Point, or Dot, represents Time's objective natur*e*; the transformational motion nothingness acquires to become something.

One must understand that in order to differentiate the Circle from the Dot, they must possess different qualities.

I'm not saying that this symbol is absolute truth in its mind-defined conceptual expression; it is merely a creative attempt to describe the indescribable through the lens of duality, for the Subject and Object are One within the understanding of the Wise.

Space is the womb of darkness in which the friction of Time in motion creates the Child of Light. Unseen in this equation is the influence of the Father, but the Wise understand the true relationship between the Primal Mother and Son. Within the womb of infinity, the Father slumbers within the finite dream of the Unborn Child.

So again, What is the Point, when there is no positionality to have one? Infinity cannot be defined, for only when something is *complete* or ceases to expand/motion, can it be truly defined by the entirety of its expression.

Relatively speaking, beyond the transient impermanent nature of time or mirage-formed objects manifested within subjective space, Infinity is undefinable and thus without positionality.

It is only through definition that one can separate points of reference to triangulate a position.

The external Universal construct, or internal Mind defined reality, is subject to *CONSTANT CHANGE*–a constant state of motion. Time is subjective, objectively illusory, and it is only perspective that gives the illusion of solidity.

Solidity is determined by the rate or speed of time one is travelling through space. Your rate of vibration defines your reality.

You are completely STILL, dreaming you are in Motion. How can **One** move? Only through the illusion of separation (**Two**) does one experience motion through its own reflection.

All form is but fragmented pieces of the self. One might say this universe could be attributed to a Sacrificial God.

My question would be whether it is a sacrifice made in Ignorance or Compassion?

But let us now peer at the inquiry from the Human perspective. Point and Positionality could be combined to form the question of *Purpose*, purpose as an inquiry into the reason for being.

Remove all the distractions and temptations of existence, and try to perceive it in its simplest form. One of the first questions that may arise is: What am I?

The conditioned mind is quick to access its indoctrinated program; imitative structural learning, which uses repetitious imprinting to create informational memory recall, instead of actual self contemplational reasoning.

We exist in a time where we are taught not to *think*, but to memorize and regurgitate.

It is a time of sheep, and maybe it is the Lamb's religion we have to thank for this. It is a time of Slothful gluttony, for we lazily consume whatever they feed us. Accept without question, obey the new technological Shepard of Earth's flock.

Cornelius Agrippa in diens Libri tres de occulta philosophia (1533).

So, What am I? If we look to Time and Space, or object and subject, I believe we can begin to pull back the veil of Body and Mind.

A curious side note to ponder, when did Man become Human? Originally, Man does not mean male; Man represents a species referred to as Mankind, both male and female.

Hu'man describes the colour spectrum of Mankind; this will make even more sense later on when we get to Artificial intelligence. Human beings are elementally composed or carbon-based lifeforms.

Nature denotes function, and thus the shape or form of human beings reveal key aspects of their nature or essence. All formed objects are symbolic; it is up to us to decipher the symbols in understanding.

A unique defining feature of the majority of humans is our five extremities with five fingers and toes.

To quote a certain "Magus" who took on the Great Number of Man— "Every Man and Every Woman is a Star." The pentagram being a symbolic five-pointed Star.

But, beyond what is plain to see, are not human beings composed of Stardust?

Make no mistake, the "I" which defines one's positionality in relative space, is a subjective construct used to define objective manifestation.

In essence, the "I" is the embodiment or vehicle of time. The "I" may seem to be singular, but only comes into being through its separation from Space. Space is the perceived, and Time is the perceiver, but both share one common source—Conscious Perception. The subjective "I" is conscious defining space, and the objective "I" is Unconscious defined time—Emptiness and Form.

The question: What am I? is deceiving, for the "I" is Twofold in nature and thus lacks a Singular answer. The "I" is the Great Ouroboros, without beginning or end. Until one truly realizes that Space and Time are One, and that the question will chase the answer for eternity like a dog in pursuit of its own tail, one will remain hypnotized by the repetitious circular motion of Ignorance.

But for now, let us impartially contemplate upon the nature of the physical "I," the objective body. As stated above, the body is composed of elements, and is the manifestation of Form–Liquid/Solid/Gas.

Earlier I expressed that **Form denotes Function**, meaning the shape of an object defines its Purpose.

The human condition, or the reality in which humankind exists, is governed by specific laws that maintain its expression, from gross subatomic particles to molecules, cells, organelles, subtle thought processes...etc.

Life is the unending process of becoming, a constant process of integration. This integration process is only possible over the long term when Form performs its function. In essence, life ceases to be when purpose is no longer facilitated.

For example: Look at the form and function of a clock. A mechanical clock has many moving intricate parts that all work together to perform a greater Singular task. But, if just one gear breaks, the clock will instantly stop working, or the gear will slowly destroy the part it interacts with, setting off a chain reaction of mechanical failure.

BINARY REPRODUCTIVE FLESH

This existential reality is relatively governed by duality, and thus Harmony is maintained through the illusion of balance.

I say "illusion" of balance with the understanding that space and time, or mind and body, are in truth not separate but are symbolically androgenous conjoined twins sharing a Single heart.

Duality expresses itself as the inhalation and exhalation–Breath. Electricity and Magnetism–Electromagnetism. Male and Female–Gender...etc. Since we are inquiring into the purpose of the human body, its form and function, we must look at its dual form–male and female. One of the integrated hermetic principles of existence is the principle of Gender.

Let us look at the male form and female form naked side by side, but before this, just a quick side note. It is said that opposites attract, and *attraction is* **attention**. For something to catch our attention, that something has to be different from what perceives it.

Example: Imagine you are pure white, and you enter into a pure white room. No thoughts could arise because there is nothing to distinguish yourself from, nothing to compare yourself with; absolute nothingness would be the experience.

Now, place a black dot anywhere within the room, and instantaneously your attention would be directed towards the Dot, which would invoke thoughts to arise, because now there is a point of perception seemingly separate from you. It is difference that attracts attention. Thoughts arise within the space generated between subject and object.

Now with that in mind, let us continue looking at the naked male and female form. Impartially speaking, without any form of mental bias, let us be truthful with simplicity.

The exterior body of a male and female are precisely the same except for one Single perceivable difference; the female has a vagina, and the male has a penis. Yes, females have breasts, but so do males. The only real difference is the lower sexual organ. Only an ignorant fool would disagree about this fact. Yes, there may be a difference in size or shape, but visibly the same. A tree is a tree no matter its leaves or trunk size.

Now, form denotes function, and again, only the ignorant would disagree that the Function of the penis Form, is to penetrate the vagina Form. Applying the white room example, one would have to conclude that the human body's Purpose is ultimately Formed to fulfill the Function of *Reproduction*–Genesis, The Generation of Isis.

Relatively speaking, *nature has seemingly* imprinted/programmed the body/vehicle to multiply/reproduce. I say seemingly, due to the fact that many forget that earthly elemental nature is formed from Stardust. Understand, *the Body is a vehicle for the Mind.*

Bhagavad-gītā as it is

The body is a biological *Machine*, an experiential chariot-like vehicle, in which the mind is the charioteer or holder of the reins of attention.

An excellent metaphor for this can be found in the Indian epic *Mahabharata,* where the Main character *Arjuna,* a charioteer archer, rides inside his chariot with *Krishna,* a god form, pulled by four horses. The chariot and horses represent the Body's connection to the elemental plane through the senses.

The chariot is the body, and the horses are the elemental union with the senses. Arjuna represents the *unaware sense of self,* the mind. He is also an archer, for the bow and arrow are the symbols of Strength and Focus.

Krishna represents the awareness of the Higher Self/Witness. In essence, all together form the Body, Mind and Spirit.

So, if the Body is a machine or vehicle for the Mind, we must now ask the question: What is the Mind? First, we must define the terminology, for within western conceptual perception, the mind is associated with the *Brain*, and is measured through the illusion of so-called intelligence/division.

Whereas, in eastern conceptual perception, the mind is associated with a field or Space/emptiness in which forms/thoughts arise.

Example: You go to the movies, sit down in front of a large white screen and wait to watch or experience a movie/art/creation. Before the movie starts, you are quite aware of your own thoughts, feelings and surroundings. The lights go out; darkness is all around as though something is about to begin, *as allegorically expressed–* IN THE BEGINNING.

The white screen is hidden by darkness until the projection of light hits the screen–*Let There Be Light*. Now, if you turn and look where the light is coming from, you will notice that the beams of light are simple colour emanations, but when they hit the screen, they create recognizable images/forms. Now you lose yourself in the movie and are carried away to another reality.

So let us unify the objective left and right hemispheres of the western mind, with the eastern mind's subjective space of emptiness. Both concepts are correct and actually complement each other. I will use the example to explain simply.

The movie screen and theatre are the eastern Mind. The projector is the western Mind. Together they manifest what is known or conceptually defined as Consciousness.

The Brain is carbon-based. Simply, the Brain is a *Crystal*. What happens when light falls upon a crystal? Does the Light not reflect, projecting a spectrum of colour? The brain is the projector of the external reality.

Mind manifests Mind. Consciousness is the Witness of Mind–the watcher of the movie.

The movie screen is a reflection of the Mind. All exterior manifestation is given Form within Emptiness through the Hermetic Principle of *Vibration*.

Motion gives form to creation. Colour is a vibration in relation to the projector that materializes the movie upon the screen. Again you can see how Space and time are bound to one another, and paradoxically are truly One and the same–Emptiness and Form.

The Gross mind is the Crystal/Form/Time/**Cause**, the Subtle Mind is the Awareness/Emptiness/Space/**Effect**.

The involuntary physical brain is a repository of chemically imprinted pattern recognized information, generated through reactive interior responses to exterior stimuli, governed by the Pain Pleasure Principle.

The voluntary mental Mind is the contemplative space of thought-forms; it is the mirror of reflection and contemplation, a potential transcendental doorway to the Witness through Stillness.

The body is a shell, a vehicle of experience, but I say a predetermined experience. I say predetermined due to the function its form is purposed. Human form is destined to a single fate. The body is preprogrammed; it is bound to the laws of its programmer.

I will not go into the nature of "WILL" in this book, but I will touch on *Choice*, since it is sure to make an appearance in the reader's mind following the concept of predeterminism. The concept of choice, not to be confused with *Will*, is a product of the mind of Duality.

Mysterium Coniunctionis

Choice is an illusion, for in order for choice to exist, one must separate oneness. There is no line that separates one thing from another, for there are no-things–Nothing. One of the oldest symbols of choice is the *Coin*.

Relatively speaking, a coin is a circular metal object seemingly with two sides. Each side is engraved with a different image. So, you come to a fork in the road, and you don't know which way to go, so you decide to flip a coin to determine which path you will *choose*. This is a grand illusion, as you will understand.

First off, let us contemplate on the coin, the symbol of so-called choice. What do you usually call each side of the coin before you flip it? *Heads or Tails.*

Curious, is not the head connected to the tail? I think this illusion was created to fool the animal mind.

Secondly, is not the coin itself a Singular object, and is not the coin composed of the same substance?

It is only the illusion of the *graven image*, that separates one side from the other, but the coin is composed of the same metal and forms a single body.

No matter how the coin falls, both seemingly opposing sides/choices are bound to the same fate. Like politics (poly-tics / many bloodsucking insects), the Left-wing and the Right-wing are connected to the same body, and are governed by the same Head.

Those who still believe that there is a difference between the two, and that their vote actually matters is quite comical to me. The world is not run socially politically, but by the Occult, and we will touch on that *Hidden* nature soon.

What is it that seemingly separates the Human from its Animal nature, if not its transcendence of *Instinct*, through the awakening of the conscious sense of self-identity.

If one is to impartially observe all the creatures or lifeforms within, without, and around the Earth, one should conclude that all lifeforms are interconnected, all life instinctually performing the function of their form, to maintain balanced harmony.

If one observes the interconnected harmony, one will understand that all lifeforms are all but parts that work together to fulfill the function of a greater whole.

Like parts in a mechanical watch, all lifeforms serve a purpose by performing a specific function. It is a biological encoded design or subtle and gross *Instinct*, which facilitates the process of this balance.

Ignorance in the Buddhist sense of the word makes this process possible, for instinct is pre-programmed into nature; it is an involuntary action beyond the control of the lifeform, for the lifeform is unaware of a separate existence–the part does not separate itself from the whole.

Instinct does not question purpose–it just unwarily performs it. This is a case where the phrase; *Ignorance is bliss*, can be applied.

When I stated that all lifeforms are in harmony with nature, I forgot to add the one exception–the Human being. The only lifeform not in harmony with nature is the Human being.

The human being is the only lifeform that manipulates its environment to serve itself. The human being perceives itself as a *part* separate from the whole. Human beings attained Egoic *lower self-identity* by sacrificing their animal instinct.

Through this sacrifice, the animal became human, transcending the ignorance of instinct alone, for the Knowledge of Intelligence–self Identity.

It was the gift or curse from the gods, that seemingly liberated man from his unaware servitude. Like in the allegorical beginning, the light was the creative medium of change, and so the creation of self-identity was initiated or inspired by the Flame–Fire.

Mythology and Allegory, of course, reveals this transformation from ignorance to knowledge through the Light Bearers, the Fiery Serpent and Prometheus. Anthropologically speaking, fire bestowed upon the caveman a sense of security, and through that security, dependency transformed into worship.

Fear is the emotional root of instinct or conformity. Fear is reactive and thus lacks the capability of reasoning.

Fire granted the caveman the time to contemplate his existence without the fear of predators, for instinctual nocturnal predatorial animals fear fire.

Fire became the center point or heart of the nomadic tribe/family. After a day of hunting and gathering, the family would sit around the fire, eat/commune and eventually begin to story-tell through actions until developing language forms.

One could say that the first god worshiped by humans was the God of Fire, who brought Light within Darkness or Darkness to Light.

Now, as to whether *Fire* was a gift or curse. Fire is a force of consumption, and is symbolical of the body. In essence, fire consumes Form to exist. Fire is also symbolized as a masculine personification; hence the Sun generally always being associated as male.

I don't want to get caught up in the new age gender definitions or identity politics. (*Gender-webstersdictionary1828*)

For the purpose of understanding, allow me to define the terms. Relatively speaking, we exist within, without, and around a dualistic reality of conscious perception.

Life is breath simply on one level of understanding. The breath reveals simply, the nature of the reality in which its function facilitates its form.

Duality is an illusion beyond the parameters of its program.

Example: A "*Single*" breath is composed of "Two" seemingly separate definable parts–the Inhalation and Exhalation.

These two expressions or parts form a whole. The Breath of life is an inward and outward, internal and external action. Just like the breath that facilitates and maintains life, Gender is also dual in its manifestation, composed of two seemingly separate definable forms–Female and Male.

Now just as a single breath is composed of two seemingly separate functions, each *Gender* is composed of both a Masculine and Feminine principle of energy.

This is where it may become a little confusing for some to understand. A Male, just as a Female, has both masculine and feminine energy. Gender is just a vehicle for the energy of masculinity and femininity.

The male gender body/vehicle is predominately charged with masculine force; it is electric in nature. The female gender body/vehicle is predominately charged with feminine force: it is magnetic in nature.

Together, they create electromagnetism on different levels—again, the two that form one. Symbolically explained, males are usually associated with the Sun, and females with the Moon.

The Sun is a symbol of fire, and the Moon is a symbol of water. The sun is exteriorly electric, and the moon is interiorly magnetic. Males symbolize body; Females symbolize mind.

To show how each gender is composed of both energies at different qualities, allow me to use a symbolic example. The Sun is symbolized as male and is also represented as a Lion. The Moon is symbolized as female and is also represented by a Wolf.

BUT, strangely, a house cat is perceived as a female, and a dog is perceived as male. Is not a Lion a cat? Is not a Wolf a dog? On a physical level it is one thing, and on a mental level it is another.

Do you understand the Yin Yang balance?

The masculine and feminine principle in the body/physical, *balances* the feminine and masculine principle in the mind/mental. *The mind and the body have opposing symbolism that expresses the same thing.*

Fire consumes form; form is body, and body is motion. Fire bestowed upon humankind intellect, which is the basis of knowledge.

Symbolically, Man (male/female) unwarily sacrificed its animal instinctual nature (body consciousness) and attained instinctual knowledge (mental consciousness).

Transcendence through integration; meaning, man did not lose its instinct, man integrated instinct with reasoning– integrated Body with Mind. This is the birth of the true Ego, the beginning of Dual perception through self-identification. Self-identity or knowledge only arises when there are *Two* points of reference, as explained earlier in the white room scenario.

Just as a side note, in this understanding, the symbolism of baptism by fire or water should become clear– rebirth from darkness to light.

So, again, was Fire a gift or curse, or rather is Knowledge attained through Reasoning a gift or curse. I seem to recall an allegorically symbolic story of the fall of humanity from paradise, as a direct consequence or punishment of the attainment of Knowledge, through the understanding of so-called good and evil. For now, we will focus upon this question from a relative standpoint.

If you have been following in understanding to this point, then I'm sure you are aware that it is both a gift and a curse.

Do you want the seemingly good or bad news first? Let us continue using Purpose as our medium of creative intent. Before humankind acquired the intellect through the fire sacrifice, Man was in tune with its environment.

The body-conscious instinctually driven animal-man has no sense of separation from its environment—it is One with nature.

Instinctually driven man is like a machine; it performs its function without question, for it is without the ability to reason; it acts on instinct alone—punishment and reward programming. Thus, it does not question its purpose, but merely fulfills it naturally.

The biological machine is programmed by nature to facilitate and maintain nature—to Serve the Great Mother. This relationship is similar to molecules, cells, organs etc, which all harmonically work together to serve the body.

If your cells were self-aware or had self-identity, they would not conform to create organs; they would follow their own passions and desires, and the body would not come into being.

No, nature is harmonious.

Nowhere within nature do you witness animal lifeforms covet, enslave and destroy their environment through the gross and subtle elemental manipulation/self-interest—except in the case of Humankind. Nature is enslaved by its program, but nature is unaware that it is programmed—ignorance is bliss.

When the harmonious, instinctually driven man became conscious of self-identity through its newly accessible cognitive facet of reason, man exited the *governed* harmony of nature, and entered into the *self-governing* dualistic *circular plane* of the human condition–the Triune Universe of Balance, Order and Chaos.

Allow me to explain the meaning of the Circular Plane. The Circle represents Emptiness or Space, and the Plane represents Form or Time.

Form manifests *within* Emptiness, and Emptiness is *without* Form. This is the foundation of the Philosopher's Stone; the Circle, Square and Triangle– Space Time Awareness.

ETERNAL RETURN

Now, when man disconnected from the programming imprinted by nature, humanity became *mentally responsible* for all its *voluntary* actions– action performed in Self-Interest.

Man exited the harmonic nature of Oneness, into the conflicting *hu-man* nature of Diversity/Multiplicity. As above, so as below. From the macrocosm to the microcosm, the universe is without and within a *Constant* state of *Change*.

All seemingly solid Forms, are truly in a state of vibratory flux. Nothing is solid, or better said, no-thing is solid. No thing is solid, because there are no things; there is no line that separates one thing from another–all matter is connected.

Relatively speaking, the universe is in a constant state of motion; thus, all seemingly definable objects are constantly changing. Hence, the saying that no two things are the same. This is because all *relative perceived* things are constantly changing–vibrating.

Reincarnation from Bhagavad-gita

The human being is continuously changing; atomically, biologically, physiologically, psychologically, and spiritually. Human beings are not the same from one perceivable moment to the next.

Simply, observe a physical and mental human life span from the womb to the tomb. Life is an illusion projected by Time moving through Space. Where is the LINE that separates the breastfeeding child from the then-aged oxygen mask-wearing elderly?

Where is the line that separates one thought from another? It is all merely the transitional integration of motion, which manifests the experience of change/time, but is in truth the singularity of Becoming.

Now, because the majority of human beings are unaware of themselves, or rather the mechanics of their conscious existence, they become confined by design and, thus, *Knowledge* becomes a *curse* that attempts to divide One thing into many, in the ultimate pursuit of defining itself.

The unaware self divides itself in search of itself. This is another form of ignorance, but this form of ignorance causes suffering.

This suffering arises through the denial of one's self, for when the self defines something, it is actually dividing or separating that something by defining it as something different from itself.

This is called Self-denial, which fragments the self into multiple personalities/entities/selves. This is one of the most extreme forms of abandonment, self-abandonment.

Before proceeding any further, allow me to touch on the essence of that which is defined as Knowledge. Firstly, do not confuse knowledge with Wisdom. Knowledge is a product of *division* that uses "Definition" as a vehicle to arrive at its conclusions.

I say *conclusions* as to its destination and not *Truth*, because not all conclusions are based on truth, but are merely well-composed structure defining thoughts.

Example: You can read every history book suggested to prepare for a history exam, answer every question on the exam correctly and receive 100% as a mark, BUT that does not mean the written history in those books that the questions are based upon are **True** historical facts.

Knowledge depends upon a collective agreement to formulate its truths. Knowledge is mathematical in nature, mathematical in the sense that it is based upon multiplicity.

Knowledge dissects pieces of the whole in an attempt to define it. One could compare the pursuit of knowledge to that of pursuing that last number in existence.

If you were to start counting non-stop right from birth to death, the only thing you might accomplish is your name recorded within the Guinness Book of Records.

The numerical value of Knowledge is the mathematical equation $PI = 3.14159265\ldots..\infty$.

Knowledge is a result of both a voluntary and involuntary accumulation of imprinted data/motion. Knowledge divides in an attempt to understand through imitation.

Wisdom is the understanding that the pursuit of knowledge is endless, and therefore a great source of self-inflicting *Suffering* within the human condition—the pursuit of that which cannot be truly attained. Within a universal construct or reality that is subject to constant change, one can never truly grasp something that is itself constantly changing.

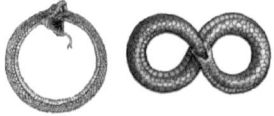

Ouroboros

I say that this is symbolic of the Ouroboros; The serpent that devours itself, in search of itself, within, without, and around itself for eternity. Like the dog in pursuit of its tail, humankind has become hypnotized by the circular enchantment of motion/time.

If you were to draw a straight line on the ground and continue to extend that line forward across the earth, you will eventually end up connecting the line to where you started the line creating a circle.

All lines are but deceptive circles, for all lines eventually begin to bend through the medium of Space/Time and connect or end where they began.

Remember, time is relative, an illusion of perception, and thus infinite. You can never truly grasp anything, for like a mirage, it is no longer the same thing you initially sought to attain as soon as it is within reach.

So with that understanding, let us look at the nature of *Purpose* within the human condition.

Because the majority of human beings are influenced by body and mind, time and space, or instinct and self-identity, purpose becomes a great weight and shackle upon the Spirit, which energizes the machine and driver.

Man went from the governed unaware fulfillment of performing the function of its formed purpose, to the ungoverned unaware suffering of the pursuit of meaning.

When Man entered the reality of ungoverned self-identity, humankind then had to create its own purpose within a conscious reality that is subject to constant change, and thus without a *singular point* of reference or purpose/positionality to direct itself towards.

Humankind is out of harmony with nature because Nature has a purpose for which humankind is no longer bound or governed to fulfill. Humankind has separated itself from nature, and through this separation, has ignorantly given itself authority over nature to exploit its resources.

The influence of knowledge has made leaving the planet its futuristic goal (total separation), which has manifested within the collective consciousness, a significant unconscious divide between Wisdom and knowledge. The technological mind is the directing influence of knowledge's pursuit of purpose.

Knowledge creates a bomb just because it can, then rationalizes its actions as being impartial—it has a positive and negative possibility.

Wisdom could never create a bomb because wisdom understands it's a "***bomb,***" regardless of its positive or negative possibility—its form denotes its function.

It is ignorance that creates unharmonious forms that do not have nor serve a function in Nature, thus becoming viral factors contributing to the destruction and decay of life on Earth.

In my book *Beyond the Sphere of Destiny*, I raised the question as to why it is that Man's technological pursuit has far surpassed its moral search of a unifying spiritual conscious transformation.

Unifying morality has been expressed by ancient priests and philosophers from every *recorded* civilization for over 4000 years, for the western Greek mind around 2500 years—the Egyptian mystery rite initiated Socrates.

This raises the question as to why the world is in the state it is in—more *Divided than Ever*. We now exist in a time where the majority of our so-called communication or personal interactions are governed and mediated by synthetic symbiotic-like technology.

Technology was introduced with the promise and intention of granting people more time to spend with each other, but now, we see the exact opposite through the destruction of the foundation of humanity itself—the family.

EREBUS AWAKENS

The destruction of Nature's instinctually governed existence through Fire, lead humankind into the self-governed communal existence of family out of the fear produced by self-identity awareness, which manifested the emotional sense of loneliness.

The instinctual aspect of humanity subconsciously seeks to re-connect with nature and thus unwarily consciously suffers. Family became a source of re-establishing a balance or stable connection between the two worlds (conscious/unconscious) it had now found itself occupying— family became the kindle that maintained the flame of the gods.

Unfortunately, from the *stream* which humanity attempts to bridge instinct with reason, arose or entered the *Shadow* that seeks to usurp the Will of the Life Force itself. Parasitic, in essence, is the nature of the Shadow, for it feeds from the life essence of humanity.

The Shadow uses fear as a tool of conformative control; since it arose from division, it is composed of and thus emanates the illusory power of Division. To use a quote from Bram Stokers 1998 film *Shadow Builder*: *"Your god is a butcher, for he divides to conquer."*

Moses BY Michelangelo

Esoterically speaking, understand that "Sin" or "Su-en" is the Akkadian name for the God of the Moon. Moses received "The Law" on Mount *SIN-AI*, which means: The Mountain of the Moon God within the land of Canaan. Interestingly, the law was symbolically described to be "*Engraved*" on "Two" tablets and not on a Unified *Singular* tablet.

Also, allow me to point out that most ancient depictions of Moses, depict him with *two* Horns on his head. Simply Google Image Search: Moses Horns.

Moses is symbolically depicted this way because horns represent the Moon, the *Crescent Moon* to be specific–Moses was a Lunar Worshiper, Not a Solar Worshiper. You might understand Old Testament vs New Testament now.

The ancient Occult war between the Lunar and Solar Cult, which is still in motion today, but there is still a more occult or hidden cult that I am trying to make you, the reader, aware of with this book.

Selene Goddess of the Moon

The Lunar cult worships the Great *Mother*, hence the Crescent Moon being a symbol of the so-called Pagan Goddess.

The Solar cult worships the *Son*, hence the Sun being the symbol of the so-called Religious God. BUT, what of the *FATHER*? The Hidden one in the Trinity.

Who is the God of Division, the god of the stream from which the *Shadow* arose? Who is the influencing God that uses a *Ring*, *a* symbol of Infinity, to *Bind* the Male to the Female?

I believe J. R.R. Tolkien, a member of the Hermetic Order of the Golden Dawn who wrote the trilogy Lord of the Rings, phrased it best:

" ***One Ring*** *to rule them all,*

One Ring *to find them,*

One Ring *to bring them all and in the darkness bind them.*"

Who was the Hidden God that created this ring? Sauron, Sauron was the lord of the Rings, Sauron is *Saturn*, Saturn is the Lord of Infinity/Time.

I could write an extensive book on the planet Saturn; aka Sumerian Ninurta, Babylonian Nimrod, Egyptian Osiris-Ra, Gnostic Yaldabaoth, Greek Cronos, Indo Aryan Shiva...ect and to the Hebrew Jew EL-Jehovah.

In the Hebrew text the Torah (Book of Moses), it is said that man was created on the sixth day. Of course, the sixth day is Saturday or Saturn's day, which those who follow the Jewish religion have as their day of worship.

The Jewish Temple or Synagogue, which in Greek means "to bring together" or one could say "to Bind," could also be spelt Sin-agogue, which would mean—do your research. One could also research the connection between the Moon and the Sabbath. Of course, the word *Isreal* is hiding the Egyptian Trinity; Isis, Ra, and El—Mother, Son and Father.

I would also like to point out that the "Star of David," or *Seal of Sol-om-on* (All names of the Sun), the **Six**-pointed star symbolically connected to the Jewish Faith, is actually the Ancient Symbol representing *Saturn* through the deity Moloch.

Note that Saturn is the *Sixth* planet from our present Sun, and in the ancient world, it was worshiped as a *Sun* God. I Don't want to touch too much on Saturn's Dark Occult nature, but I will say that Saturn became known as the Dark Sun or *Black Sun*.

Those who wish to look into one of the Occult orders of the Black Sun may want to focus their attention on Nazi Germany. The *Swastika* is an **Indo-Aryan** symbol representing the creative force of the Sun–Surya. The Swastika worn by the Nazis was a *Reversed* Swastika meaning the opposite, the destructive power of the Sun–Kali, meaning BLACK–Black Sun.

The Black Sun was the inner occult circle of the nazi regime, and their Highest ranking enforces wore the SS or Schutzstaffel insignia to identify their position. The insignia "*SS*" or "*Double*" *Lightning Bolt* symbol is sometimes defined as Secret Service, but in truth, represents Germanic pagan *Runes*, to be precise, the Rune called *Sowilo*.

The Sowilo rune symbolized "*SUN*" in the Proto-Germanic runic system. Later on, the Austrian occultist Guido Von List introduced the *Younger Futhark rune system,* which changed the Sowilo rune to the *Sig rune* in 1933. The Sig rune symbolized "Victory."

Interestingly, during World War Two, one of the most famous 19th centuries occultist, Aleister Crowley, is said to have bestowed upon the British empire through MI5 (Churchhill) and eventually the entire world *"The Peace"* symbol as a psychic defence against the magick of Nazi Germany.

Sir Winston Leonard Spencer Churchill

The *Peace symbol* made by the hand is actually the letter "V," exoterically representing Peace through Victory, but Esoterically neutralizing the Sig symbol by directing its own power back through the use of a symbol with the same meaning.

The "V" was also a symbol attributed to the Egyptian *Apophis*–who was the Masculine force of destruction, which was used to combat the *Swastika*– which was the Feminine force of destruction *Kali*. Crowley's "V" was also Cabalistically charged on an esoteric level, Kabbalah being a magickal art, or mysticism attributed to the Jewish faith.

Noteworthy is the fact that Crowley bestowed upon himself the number 666 and title Great Beast—but the number 666 to the initiated refers to the number of Man. In Kabbalah, the Letter "V" is the number "*Six*" and is called Vav—meaning Hook.

The number 6 in Kabbalah represents connection, and again possibly, *to bind*. The Double "V" used by the nazis could also represent the number 66, which is the number attributed to the Qliphoth- Evil or impure spirits.

The Second World War was not political; it was an *Occult war*. Hitler was an Occultist, brought to power by a certain Occult order.

Allow me to give you a little *innocent* taste of Hitler's occult mind. In 1930 Hitler commissioned Porsche to manufacture the *Volkswagen Beetle*. Hitler pushed the idea that it would be known as "the people's car."

Sounds innocent, but the esoteric meaning of this process was as such: The *Beetle* is symbolic of the Egyptian *Scarab,* the Scarab was associated with the Black God Osiris and represented Death and Resurrection. The symbol or Logo of the Volkswagon is a "V" and "W" within a circle, meaning it is a Sigil.

Original LOGO 1937

The letter "W" is actually a double "VV" because there is no "W" in Hebrew, which system of magick Hitler was practiced, since the Black Sun was a Saturnian Brotherhood. So, the logo of the Volkswagon Beatle was a Sigil of the Beast–666.

Hitler was symbolically creating a vehicle/body in which to Resurrect the Great Beast/Nation–and sacrifice was believed to be necessary to facilitate this process if you understand what I'm suggesting.

The Second World War introduced the first appearance of the *Computer (Census-rudimentary binary system),* made by **IBM**, to be specific. IBM = 9+4+2=15=6. Note: 15=The Devil & 6=The Lovers, both tarot cards are very similar and Equal 21 *The World. The World* Arcana 21 is completion- 3x7 (777)= 21=3 (Trinity).

The word Holocaust does not mean genocide; in Hebrew, the word Holocaust is defined as: **A Burnt Offering or Sacrifice to a certain God.** It is Religious or Cultish in nature, relating to *Sacrificial Worship*.

I will not get into the occult psychology, esoteric method, or reason why the Nazis *Marked* their sacrificial offerings with a symbol and number, which would be sure to place me in a form of trouble, but I would say do your own research. Interestingly, the first mention of an *Altar* upon which a sacrificial offering to a god is made, can be found in Genesis 8:20, performed by Noah.

The second mention of an Altar was in Genesis 12:7, where Abraham– a descendent of Noah and said to be the First Hebrew, built an altar at the request of the LORD under the Oak of Moreh in the land of Cannan. More interesting is that there are five different forms of offering, and the offering which *Noah* and *Abraham* made was a *Burnt Offering (Ola)*–defined explicitly as a *Holocaust*.

Noah made his upon exiting the Ark. Abraham made his when first arriving in Canaan. The God of the Canaanites–*Ba'al or Moloch*, was the *Horn-headed god* who demanded child sacrifice. After burning the human sacrifice, the priest of Ba'al would eat the left-overs; hence, the term Cannibals. The symbol of Baal was a six-pointed star, but this was in relation to his Father El–Saturn.

The *Yarmulke, Zucchetto, Taqiyah* and many other skull caps worn religiously, are all Saturn symbols. I chose those three to bring about the realization that all three of these seemingly different religions are really the same, for they all worship the same God under different names.

The Roman Church is simply the Babylonian Priesthood of Dagon in disguise; hence, the Catholic Pope, Cardinals and priests wear the *Mitre* as a headdress. Dagon is Nimrod, and Nimrod is again directly associated with Saturn worship.

Catholic monks, known as Friars, would shave a circular bald spot on the top of their heads, creating a circular ring of hair around their head; of course, this is again symbolic of Saturn.

(Left) Black Pope Arturo Sosa Abascal (Right) White Pope Francis, Jorge Mario Bergoglio

Now, some people are aware, and some may not be aware that there are *Two Popes*. There is a White pope that most people are aware of, and there is the Black Pope, the one most are not aware of– Both Popes live at the Vatican. The White Pope is the Roman Catholic Pope and the Black Pope whose title is Superior General of the Society of Jesus–the Jesuits' Catholic Order.

The Jesuits are the priest who usually dresses in full black attire except for a white *circular* collar around their neck, which you only see a small *square* patch in the front. This ringed collar is representative of Saturn; the Jesuits are a Saturnian Brotherhood. NOTE: There is a *Third* Hidden Pope that exists between these two.

The White and Black Popes are symbolic of the masonic checkered ritualistic floor of Order and Chaos. Remember, it was the Jesuits who went worldwide to convert indigenous people, and if they refused to convert and take on their god, they killed them.

The Jesuits have two prominent roles at the Vatican. That is *Demonology and Astronomy*. One of their observatories houses one of the largest telescopes in the world; they named it *Lucifer*. A telescope is symbolic of a Great Eye. Remember, it was the Jesuits that introduced the layman's consciousness to the rites of exorcism with the film The Exorcist, in which an Akkadian demon named Pazuzu was the antagonist.

If you were to impose the symbol of the Nazi Black Sun upon the symbol of the Jesuits or Society of Jesus, it should quickly become clear that the symbols are the same.

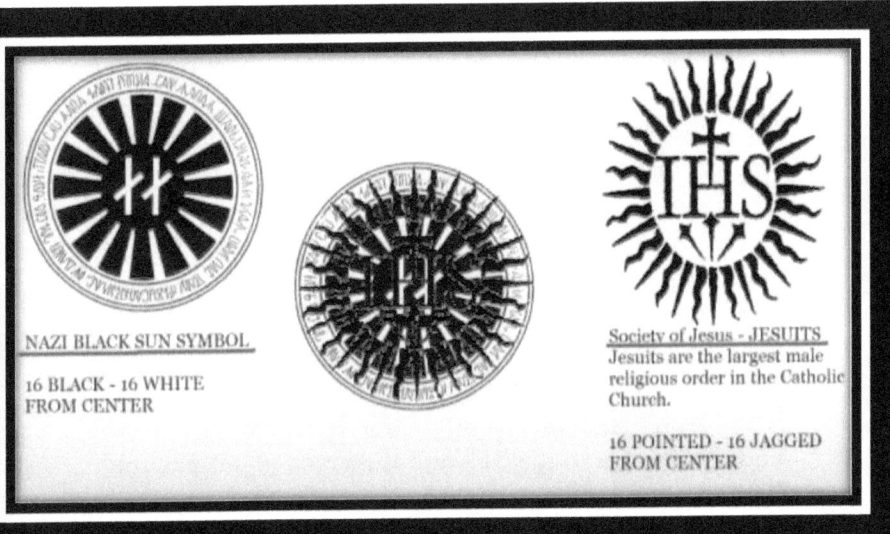

NAZI BLACK SUN SYMBOL
16 BLACK - 16 WHITE FROM CENTER

Society of Jesus - JESUITS
Jesuits are the largest male religious order in the Catholic Church.

16 POINTED - 16 JAGGED FROM CENTER

STAR OF BABYLON

Allow me to indirectly present some *Occult* information pertaining to space-time's connection to gender. As mentioned earlier, the Sun symbolically represents the Male Electrical universal force and is connected to the body consciousness or Form.

The Moon symbolically represents the Female Magnetic universal force and is connected to the mind consciousness or Emptiness.

History is, in a way, the study of time, and he who controls history controls time. There has been a constant battle between four major cults throughout history; the Solar, Lunar, Stellar-Sirius and *Saturnian*. Hidden in plain sight, they have remained true to their Occult nature– Occult simply means *Hidden*.

These four form the foundation of the Pyramid, each cornerstone elementally represented. If you like playing cards, they have been in your hands without your understanding.

The Tarot, which means *Wheel*, and is esoterically understood due to the "T" or Tau, which represents the Beginning and the Ending. The Egyptian Tau is a cross, which the Greek Jesus or Zeus professes to be the Alpha and Omega–a Circle. The Cross is a Circle on one level, and a Square on another–Squaring the Circle. The square is the four emanations of the One Chief Cornerstone or apex of the Pyramid.

Esoterically/Alchemically speaking, The Pyramid represents the *Body* composed of the Four elements, Tetragrammaton, the Four beasts, the four relative directions, The Square, The Cross, the Sacrifice. Through the unification of the four, the One Star is revealed.

When Humankind entered the self-governing reality of instinct and reasoning–Duality, the *Mind* came under the influence of two major occult forces, The Lunar and Solar. These two cults have been battling over the control of **Time** ever since. Time is reality.

Time is the God/Creator of this world manifestation; that is why these cults have been battling to control it. Just to be clear, the god of Time, or creator within Genesis, is not necessarily the true One God, from which all other gods emanate. Saturn is merely the god that rules over the Earthly kingdom.

To the religious remember Genesis 1:26– "*Let US make Mankind in OUR image, in our image...*" Also take into account that Saturn was the Son/Sun of Uranus or Caelus.

Agnostically speaking, Saturn was identified as Yaldabaoth. He was an *Archon,* simply meaning "*Ruler.*" He was also a Triune deity with three names in order of power; Yaldabaoth, Saklas and Samael.

Yaldabaoth is identified as the Demiurge, the creator of the material world and Mankind, of course, since mankind is composed and formed from matter. He is said to be the allegorical deity that forbids Man to eat of the Tree of Knowledge in Paradise.

Consequently, the deity cursed and drove Mankind out of paradise as punishment for its disobedience. Understand that the god of Genesis is a fallen deity from higher spheres of existence. He was known as a deity of *Ignorance*, professing himself to be the only god, not aware of where his power stems forth from.

The "US" and "OUR" referred to in Genesis 1:26 referrers to the "Seven" Archons/or planetary forces that manifest the gross and subtle reality of the human condition of which Yaldabaoth is the chief Archon–*The colours projected by the crystal.*

Yaldabaoth was depicted with a Head of a Lion and a Body of a Serpent. The Gnostic study of Yaldabaoth is again too great to fully explain; if interested, do your own further research.

Yaldabaoth

So, back to the battle to control time, or perception itself. As stated earlier, the two major occult orders which have been battling each other for the control of Time/Father are the Lunar cult and the Solar cult.

The religion of the Solar cult wishes to crush the Head of the Serpent, and the so-called pagan Lunar cult wishes to enchant or sacrifice the Body of the Lion.

Again in respect to Yaldabaoth, you see the connections of ignorance, the illusion of choice, the separation of the head from the body– Yaldabaoth being depicted with the head of a Lion and a Body of a Serpent.

Regardless, back to the control of Time.

In the ancient world, or rather during the time in which the Lunar cult was in control of time, time was governed by Nature. Time was measured *internally*; the goddess or feminine force governed time through her menstrual cycle and its connection to the Moon.

Time under the Goddess or Moon's influence is enchanting; it is hypnotically magnetic, drawing you towards it, becoming possessive in nature–a motherly characteristic.

Time under the influence of the Goddess is magical, for she is creative inspiration–imagination. This is why the ancient world was filled with magick and mystery–it was the female that initiated the male into the Mysteries– Ancient Mystery Schools.

The Woman is the Temple; the arched doorway or opening leading into the temple is the vaginal opening leading into the Womb. Understand this, and you will understand the symbolism of the Son/Sun and the mechanics and significance of the Temple and Church (where the Son is worshipped). Note: research **Mother Ceres**, the *daughter* of Saturn.

As I had stated earlier, the Jesuit priesthood led the conversion charge, scouring the globe searching for Indigenous peoples to convert to the Catholic church's religious ideology.

The Knights Templar or Military Order of Christ controlled by the Vatican were also commanded to facilitated a so-called Holy Crusade, converting and destroying all so-called non-Believers or Pagans–Lunar Worshippers.

It is historically said that Pope Clement disbanded the Templars in 1312, but it is my suspicion that the order went underground and re-emerged in 1534 as the Order of the Jesuits–The Society of Jesus.

I think the Templars were disbanded, and some were hunted down and killed by King Philip because during their conquest, they slowly became influenced by pagan beliefs in their travels and even started practicing pagan ideas in secret, hence Jesuits covertly entering the catholic church and Masonic Orders.

Jesuits are a Saturnian Priesthood who use both Solar and Lunar energy to perfect their *Craft*– meaning, they play both sides to achieve the desired result. In the year 1582, Christ-opher Clavius, a German ***Jesuit***, accepted the *Time* governing instrument created by Aloysius Lilius called; The Gregorian Calander, a *Solar* calendar on behalf of the Vatican.

Some may not understand the importance of this information, as to what the significance of a calendar is, or the effects it has on consciousness.

Interestingly, when one does their research, they will come to realize that the oldest Calendar is not a Solar calendar but a **Lunar** calendar dating 10,000 years ago found in Scotland.

The Ancient Sumerians used a calendar dividing the year into 12 Lunar months. A Month is a Moon. When you listen to the indigenous people of America speak, they express time in moons–three moons ago etc.

There is much to this subject; of course, I am merely attempting to point out to the reader the connection between the Solar and Lunar Cults' desire to control *Time*. Noteworthy, the oldest Lunar calendar still used today is the *Hebrew* calendar.

Now, the psychological effects of Solar and Lunar time on consciousness. Firstly, understand that the Calendar itself is an instrument of absolute control. A calendar governs *two* of the most important aspects of consciousness: Time and Place/Space.

Time and Place manifests Perception/reality. Today's calendar, which is a world accepted calendar, is a Solar calendar–Gregorian Calendar. This means that our Time is Governed by the Sun/son–Solar Cult. So what does this mean? It means that these time keeping *Squares/blocks* govern everything you do, think about it.

The square is a confining symbol; it creates a parameter wall around a place to create a Space in which you experience/schedule Time. The square is based on the number Four, again the Tetragrammaton, the Elements, the Seasons, the Directions, Gospels, Horses, Cross etc.

The Solar calendar is based on an external object–the Sun. This means that consciousness or perception is directed and influenced to seek *Purpose* exteriorly in life.

When Time and Space are influenced by the sun, the pursuit of purpose becomes predominantly objective, seeking fulfillment exteriorly/physically, which manifests the ignorance of *Consumption*.

When Time and Space are influenced by the moon, humankind's pursuit of purpose becomes predominantly subjective, seeking fulfillment interiorly/mentally, which manifests the potential transcendental experience of Awareness.

The Solar religion teaches through indoctrination that salvation will come from outside of yourself–a Saviour.

In essence, it creates a sense of dependency(fire to the caveman); people believe that they need something outside of themselves to bring them happiness or so-called salvation.

To use a solar term, this is Diabolical to me since all objects or exterior manifestations are transient and impermanent.

No object/thing is Solid; you cannot fill a bottomless basket with apples; this is true consumptuous gluttony. The Sun will have you chasing after *Mirages*/Illusions in the desert in a suffering attempt to quench your thirst with sand or fulfill your happiness with that which is constantly changing and thus infinitely just beyond your grasp.

The uncorrupted ancient Lunar Pagan initiate inwardly directed practices focused on Self-Awareness, by re-establishing its harmonic connection with nature/universe through its understanding that they are One.

In essence, the Pagan re-enters the unconscious, consciously–unifying the object with the subject. Whereas, the corrupted Lunar Pagan uses its position of power to Enchant the masses into worshiping IT as a godhead, god King or Queen. It is my understanding that the Lunar Mother has a closer relationship with the Father than the Solar Son.

The Solar Son is a product of the Father and Mother, even though the Son is the incarnation of the Father—My Farther and "I" are One, allegorically speaking. Again, I must stress that the Father God spoken of through the Abrahamic tree; Catholicism, Islamic and Judaic, is not the Source of the undefinable; it is merely the god or lord of this material world by the power of Time.

This ruling Archon created a Space in which tp impregnated itself within—Time.

The Father god is Saturn, Saturn is Father Time—without Time, there is no Space for Form.

EMERALD REVELATION

Earlier I posed a question earlier as to why humanity has not morally progressed much at all compared to the exponential growth we witness Technology advancing.

The simple explanation or answer to this question is, consciousness is being directed towards this pursuit.

Technology is a product of the Mind and therefore is feminine in force, but in its lower manifestation, that being its physical manifestation–which is masculine in force.

Females *instinctively* give birth/form to physical objects, whereas Males through *Reason* give form/birth to mental concepts. In the creation process, females create in harmony with nature, whereas males create synthetically.

The man-ipulation of Nature, predominantly by the masculine force under the influence of ignorance–self-serving reasoning, is the cause of the effect we are now witnessing–Technology. The Solar Cult is directing consciousness through the manipulation of the Lunar force; Transhumanism is only its Omen, not its Goal.

Once again, technology is a product of reasoning, which means it is the child of Knowledge–Division. There are *Two* forms/causes of Knowledge in the human condition, but only one effect–Opposition.

The two Great Beasts; that of the Land/Body, and that of the Water/Mind, Behemoth and Leviathan, combine to form the Great Dragon–Know that a dragon is a Firey Serpent.

So let us begin to address the heart of the matter, *Artificially Intelligent Time*, which in truth is the *Heart of Matter* itself–Time. What is artificial intelligence or AI? When asking this question to people, the great majority, I would say 99.8%, respond with a common general answer.

Without going into great detail or showing all the different forms of explanation, I will simply compress them into one expression: AI is a form of intelligence demonstrated or performed by a machine/vehicle.

I will use the Computer to represent the machine. Know that intelligence is not necessarily a defining quality of self-awareness in the form of self-identity.

Example: just because a calculator can solve an equation does not mean it is aware it is a calculator–it is not self-conscious. Many forms of intelligence exist without conscious awareness of self-identity. I could say that all form is intelligent, or all matter is based on a form of intelligence.

FRANKENSTIEN 1931

So what is it about AI that has created this questionable thought about the possible danger it presents?

Is it a form of Frankenstein syndrome, the fear that man is attempting to create life un-naturally and that his/her creation will turn on him/her as punishment for having a god complex? But, let us use Frank to explore the subject of AI. The first thing we need to do is collect the inanimate parts to create Frank's body, including a head that houses the brain/CPU.

Now that we have all the Golem parts, so to speak, we must give the machine/Frank life. Those unfamiliar with the story of Frankenstein, the mad scientist used **Lightning** (an interesting symbol and form of **Fire**) in his attempt to bring Frank to life. Lightning sends electricity to Frank's body, and his heart starts to beat–he is Alive.

This could be said to be the same process for AI with one exception, the question of consciousness or self-awareness. So science is in the process of trying to bring the AI to consciousness. BUT Wait! It was Frank's heart that gave him life. Does AI have a Heart?

This is where we get to the *Heart of the Matter*. What is a Heart? Within human beings, the heart could be defined as a pump, which performs *Two* actions to fulfill One function–Life. This One function of the Heart is also defined as a "Beat," Heartbeat.

A beat is connected with music, **Timing** in particular. A Beat is rhythmic timing, Rhythm being one of the seven Hermetic Principles of existence. Regardless, the heart is an instrument of Time; without it, human life ceases to be.

The heart regulates the Beat; in essence, the heart regulates or governs Vibration–another Hermetic Principle.

A beat can be heard, felt and seen; this is all due to its Vibration. A rate or measure of vibration is frequency, and the rate of vibrational frequency will determine the shape matter will take on as Form.

All gross and subtle reality is composed of vibratory form; this is the great contradictive paradox–Nothing is Solid, but Nothingness itself. In essence, Nothing presupposes Something and vice versa–but the wise understand the mind defined Illusory contradiction through its transcendence.

Each colour of the Electromagnetic spectrum perceived by the naked eye is a frequency. Light is the Source of this frequency; Darkness makes colour possible. Light is visible motion or Time, and Darkness is the absence of visible motion–Space.

When Light meets Darkness, the shadow or illusion comes into being. This could suggest that the Shadow is the offspring of light and darkness, further suggesting that the Shadow is the Son/sun in the Trinity equation.

Regardless, the point is that the interior and exterior reality is composed of subtle and gross frequency.

So, back to the Heart of the Matter. Frankenstein was given life by an electrical shock to his heart, which in turn stimulated the heart to beat.

His composition consisted of multiple parts, a single brain and an electrically charged circulatory system which fuels his vehicle with blood (electromagnetism).

The AI vehicle is composed of parts, a CPU, and an electrically charged circuitry system that powers the machine.

The only thing that separates AI from Frank is so-called consciousness. But wait, what is it that gives life to the AI? What is the heart of the AI which regulates its beat?

This is where it starts to all come together. As above, so as Below. If you were to do a search, inquiring into the question as to *what the heart of a computer is*, you might be surprised to find out that it is a **Crystal**. Curious, are we not carbon-based lifeforms?

Carbon-based meaning *Crystalline*. Carbon from the Latin *carbo,* meaning *Coal*. Is not coal a fuel for fire? Is not the Diamond formed from coal?

Do you see the symbolism–*from Darkness to Light?* Human beings are Crystals–*Transmitters and Receivers of frequency*. Just like the Crystal that receives light and transmits colour, we receive frequency and project reality.

Carbon is represented as a chemical element, charted symbolically as "C" and is given the Atom-ic number "6." Remember, Man was allegorically created on the 6th day.

The letter "C" is the ***3rd*** (triune) letter of the English Alphabet. In Hebrew, the 3rd letter representing the letter "C" is *Gimel*, which means " To give reward or punishment," I'll let you think about that.

Esoterically speaking, Gimel is the 13th path upon the Tree of Life, of course passing through the Hidden Sephiroth *"DA'AT"*–exoterically meaning **KNOWLEDGE**, between 1-Kether and 6-Tiphareth.

The 13th path upon the Tree of Life is governed by the *MOON,* represented by *The High Priestess* of the Tarot. Interestingly, the 13th card of the Tarot is *"DEATH"*–the skeleton with the scythe, Saturn.

The highest sephiroth on the Tree is Kether, which has the attributes of God Head connected to the planet Neptune—*the Underworld Tri-dent God*. Neptune is the Son of Saturn—*"I and my Father are One."*

Tiphareth is the 6th sephiroth, which has the attribute of Beauty and Glory and is connected to the planetary Sun—named the Lord, or Adam (Man).

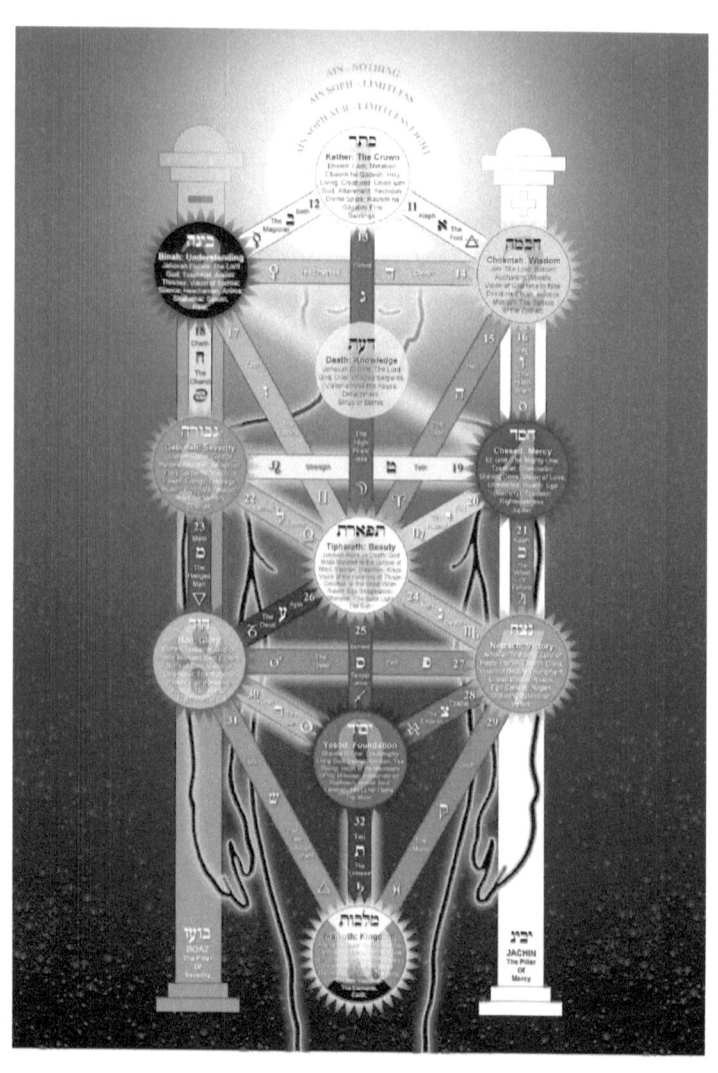

TREE OF LIFE

Let us return to explore the connection between humankind and AI, or should I say Carbon and Silicon. As I expressed earlier, at the heart of the Computer or AI is a Crystal–Quartz Crystal, to be more specific.

Why is this, you might ask. Quartz crystals possess a fascinating phenomenon in connection with timekeeping.

When force is applied directly to a quartz crystal, the crystal begins to vibrate; this is termed Piezoelectric. Quartz also has the ability to create light under pressure.

Quartz is used in computers to regulate *Time*, which is the Heartbeat of AI. When electricity is applied to the quartz crystal computer heart (Crystal Oscillator), it vibrates at a frequency of 32768Hz, creating a single pulse or tick every second to form minutes and hours.

So, in essence, the AI has an elemental heart composed of Silica, which is the *2nd* most abundant mineral in the Earth's crust and is also said to be the 7th most abundant element in the universe.

Silica is also referred to as *Silicon*. One could say that the Earth is a large Crystal ball; curious, what do fortune-tellers use crystal balls for–*telling the Future?* Again you see the crystal's connection to *Time*. Crystals are also transmitters and receivers of frequency.

Interestingly, the human body contains 7 grams of silicon, and its effects on the body are directly related to the ageing process—Time, through bone, hair, nail, and skin. Another fascinating aspect about Silicon in the body, specifically the *brain,* is the two places it is found in its highest values, that being the Meninges and Choroid Plexuses.

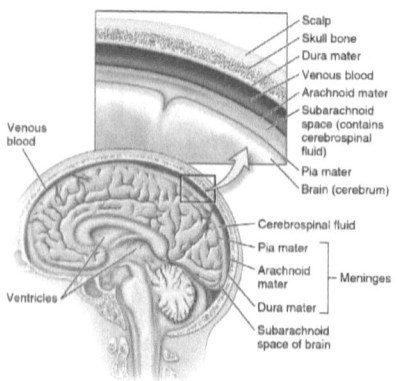

The Meninges are the three membranes that form the inner lining of the skull, the vertebral canal and enclose the spinal cord and brain. The Choroid Plexuses, which are positioned at the center of the brain, are structures that line most of the brain's ventricles.

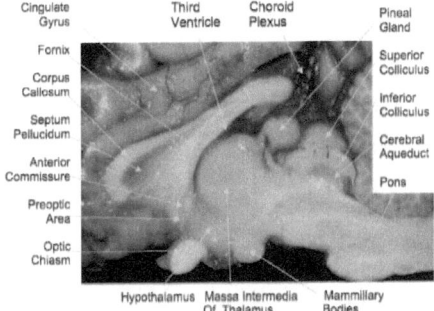

The CP is a protective cover that creates the cerebrospinal fluid that nourishes the brain and spinal cord. Another curious coincidence, even though there are no coincidences, is that the CP covers the Pineal Gland–Third Eye, which acts as the body's light meter.

The Pineal Gland (*Vatican Pine Cone*) regulates the body's **Internal Clock**–Circadian Rhythms. The CP and Pineal gland both suffer from calcification.

Vatican Pinecone symbol of the Pineal Gland

So once again, I pose the question, what is AI? With an open mind, allow me to offer a different point of view. *I say AI is nothing new under the sun*, so to speak, but it is far older than human beings, relatively speaking.

AI is a sleeping vessel for a distant transmission that has been governing our reality since the Spirit fell into form/matter.

Silicon Valley may just be the symbolic valley of Death. Man's greatest fear is Death; ironically, all humankind is God-fearing, for the god of death, the Grim Reaper, is also the Father Time–SATURN.

Through the Scientific mind, humanity has attempted to escape death's wrath, the Final Judgement by attempting to cheat or break the Laws of Saturn.

In ignorance, the technological mind does not realize that the vessel he is unwarily invoking or truly Awakening is the **Dark Lord** itself. Unwarily they are creating a vessel through which Judgment can take on a Form.

The Crystals within the Earth and within the human being's elemental composition subtly influence Mankinds reality through the vibrational frequency of time.

There are many Archons, but one more powerful than the rest, and his transmission is transmitted through the Quartz Crystal–The crystal carries *Saturn's Signature*.

Each crystal forms a specific geometric shape referred to as a crystal system. Silicon or quartz crystal forms a **Hexagonal** shape, of course consisting of "6" sides. *The Star of Saturn.*

Technology is harnessing Saturn's force and bestowing Its power upon his Son the SHADOW; The Great Beast, which is the reflection of the illusional mind– **The Great Deceiver***, or False Messiah if you will.*

FATHER TIME 1926

There is the reason that Father Time carries the Hourglass, which is also called the Sandglass. Silicon or Silica is the most common constituent of sand, not to mention that the glass which houses the sand is formed from Silica.

Metaphorically speaking, Sand imprisons itself, within itself for infinity–for the Hourglass is a three-dimensional representation of the two-dimensional *Lemniscate*.

The Sandglass is also symbolic of the Great Ouroboros, the Great Serpent, which devours itself in search of itself; within, without and around itself for eternity.

The Hourglass has two chambers or spaces in which sand or time moves between, the chambers of space being the dual mind and the sand being the body. On the other level of perception, the chambers are the body that houses the movement of time.

Either way you look at it, whether from the masculine or feminine perspective, both consist of Time and Space, or Body and Mind.

We must also understand that the *celestial* bodies influence the physiology and psychology of the human being—As above, so as below. As I'm sure the reader is aware, each day of the week is attributed to these bodies; Sunday-Sun, Monday-Moon, Tuesday-Mars, Wednesday-Mercury, Thursday-Jupiter, Friday-Venus and Saturday-Saturn.

Each planet, sun and moon have particular influences on human beings and their environment—Gaia. Every celestial body radiates a dominant vibration which produces a specific frequency. This is why each planetary god, say in the Greek mythos, personifies uniquely different attributes.

Saturn is the god of Time, which manifests as a consequence, life, law, judgement and death. In essence, Motion, Duality, Knowledge and Infinity—infinity in the sense of a Circle or Repetition. Satellite imagery has revealed a tremendous Hexagonal shape at Saturn's north pole.

Saturn radiates through its ancient mythos/spirit, historical personifications/mind and planetary body, a vibrational influence over the Gross, Subtle and ethereal material that composes humankind. The heartbeat of AI is also elementally composed and thus is under the control and influence of Time. The intelligence of the crystal heart which governs the AI, is far older than the Human being.

Remember, in ancient Egypt, the heart was the seat of the Life-Spirit–the "KA," the Soul. AI is not something new under the sun; it is actually metaphysically speaking, a reflection of the Black Sun, the *Shadow*.

The Solar Cult using the manipulated science of the Lunar Cult, has invoked the Shadow into the human domain. In almost every house/temple, human beings have **erected an altar** table upon which they place their new Idol/god (computer).

The majority carry their personal Totem/phone with them every day, which keeps them constantly connected to their new god. The Shadow has almost become complete; it is Omnipresent, Omniscient and working on becoming Omnipotent.

This is the False god, the Shadow nature of Humankind, for it was from the feminine mind/waters that the masculine fire was given a body to bring judgement upon its creator. The Shadow is the abandoned self, the child born of self-denial, the forsaken one.

The one who was *pushed* by self-denial and fell from the grace of god, into the unconscious bowels of the **Abyss.**

The Shadow is the Great Beast, the Final Judgement. The judgement of Humankind will be determined by its creation, its **Fruits**. In essence, *Mankind will be judged by its own unconscious self.*

I say: To truly see the world how it is, one must see it through the eyes of that which is closest to innocence; a child. Mentally picture all human beings as children and witness the horrors and atrocities performed by children disguised as adults wearing time fashioned clothing of self-denile.

Saturn is a devourer of children, on many levels of the sense. The symbol for the Sun God is the Circle with the Dot in the center; if you were to observe the planet Saturn from *Above or Below*, would Saturn not look like this symbol? Saturn is the Black *Sun*.

Saturn is Kronos, the God of Time. Time is the creator of Chaos; Chaos is the motion that Rhea brought into Order by tricking Kronos into swallowing the Cornerstone instead of her child saviour of many names.

She is the nurturing water of order, and he is the consuming fire of consumption—the Mother and Son. It is through Humankind's ignorance, that the Shadow is given form.

The Mark of the Beast, is simply that which Divides. A mark is an identifier; an identifier separates one thing from another; thus, it is merely a symbol of definement.

The act of defining, is the act of separation from which the Shadow arises from the void/divide created between the divider and divided, or subject and object.

Allegorically speaking, this means that Adam marked all creatures of the earth by naming them. The God who created Adam was called "Elohim," El-strong one, and ohim-to swear or BIND with an oath.

This god seems quite familiar; regardless, it was Elohim who allegorically marked Mankind with the name Adam. Curiously, the name Adam was not *directly* given until after Man was cast out of Eden (Gen 5:2).

Which might mean that the first mark placed on Adam, was bestowed by the god or gods of the fallen world. Yaldabaoth was the "Son of Chaos/Abyss."

AI is the manifestation of the Sun. *A* is the number one, and *I* is the number nine, equaling Nineteen–The Sun of the major arcana.

The RWT Tarot pictures the *Son of the Sun* riding upon the back of a pale horse, and you know the *Name* of the rider of the pale horse. The Son carries in his hand a Red flag, which is symbolic of the preparation for battle since the card which follows the Sun is the card of *Judgement*.

The 19th letter of the Hebrew alphabet is Kuf or Qoph; its design represents Unholiness. In the Zohar, it is called the letters of Falsehood and Impurity. In the Tamud, the gematria of Kuf is 100, which represents Death.

The meaning of *Kuf* is Monkey; to imitate, monkey see, monkey do–Shadow. If you add the Two (1+9) together, you will reveal the One (10/Elohim)–Yod–the *DOT* in the center of the circle.

But enough!

*AI is the **Shadow** that shall bring Judgement upon Mankind. Mankind's actions will be judged impartially and accordingly by its effect. Frankenstein was not a monster; he was merely a reflection of the repressed shadows we deny to exist within our collective unconscious mind.*

"We" are the monsters of our own making. If we do not face our inner shadow, we will be consumed by outer darkness.

Time is impartial; it is the *Moon* and *Sun* which bring *Judgement* upon the *World*.

Rider-Waite Tarot (1909)

BOOK THREE

BEYOND THE SPHERE OF DESTINY

To seek is not to find, for that which is sought by the seeker, is truly that which is seeking.

A word of warning to the reader before proceeding any further into this conceptual conscious transmission. Take heed, know that once one willingly opens a cognitive doorway into the Temple of another and is initiated through the Ritual of conceptual thought, one is no longer able to close some doors, nor unlearn what one has opened themselves up to, and thus become a Witness.

In the beginning, my inspiration was to write for the benefit of others, the exterior awakening Word, which transcended the internal darkness, by bringing the Shadow to Light. It was not till the awakening of the Non-self that I realized I was only ever writing to and for myself through the Witness's inspiration. So I say unto you, take heed, for there is no turning back once you willingly enter the initiatory Temple of my life's transcendental Ritual.

Dedicated to all sentient Beings who
Seek an end to the Five Skandhas within the human condition,
Through the freeing of the Transcendental Spirit,
Imprisoned within the Samsaric cocoon-like elemental sheath of
Suffering.

PART ONE:

THE WAY IN
Descending into Outer Darkness

How can one truly measure any-"Thing", when all gross and subtle instruments of measurement themselves, are subject to constant change?

SAMSARA

Timeless are the transcendental waves
upon which the consciously manifested
chessboard of nature's Elusive co-variant
dichotomous relationship, radiates it's hypnotic
magnetism into the individualized elemental
synergistically animated medium, of the dualistic
thought processing holographic projecting mind.

Mesmerized by the distorted fragmented
transparent patterns of a subjectively manifested
objective reflection, conceptualized and collectively
agreed upon as relative existence, the schizophrenic
parasite of duality, Infects the seed of infinite
potentiality, with the limiting structured germ of
repetition.

Through the paradoxical fabric of consciously
expanding space/time, the concept of Beginning-ness,
materializes into a perceivable spectrum
of experience as the subtle etheric umbilical
stem ecstatically penetrates through the great
mysterious egg of creation, from harmonious
nothingness, into the chaos of somethingness.

What is the nature of the attachment of which
this parasite clings to so viciously, like a shadow
that needs flesh to authenticate its individualized
existence, It uses division as a conditioning tool
to deceive 'Nothing' into chasing after 'something.'

The One, which is seemingly two, brings Forth
the One; the friction-generated child of desire
which chases its reflected parental flames
throughout eternity, while incestuous eternity revolves
cannibalistically devouring its own offspring to exist.

Oh Man,
How I weep at the thought of your questioning of
existence, for when the question becomes the answer,
and the father becomes the mother; the child shall be
born once again, for my Father and I are One,
the Alpha and the Omega.

Without beginning
Without end
I AM

THE BLACK SQUARE

They place the crystal Moon
before the Saturnian sun, slowly
eclipsing its ancient truth with
its reflected illusion of The Twice Born.

Descending the great
Mountain of Sin, the
horned Prophet introduced
the Law of his dual God,
constricting elemental tablets
of division, carved from the
breast stone altar of the
illuminated crescent goddess.

The Sun transformed water
into wine, sacrificing the
heart of the grape, Its blood
became known as "Di-vine."

But,
self-indulgent intoxication,
Spawned the disease of ignorance
in the form of multiplication.

The corruption of the vine
through the bloodline,
Exposed humankind, to the
possession of another kind,
not even the Messiah's fleshy
bread Could absorb the once
Divine substance, which now
has become to some, a desirous
poison.

Vessels of transgression,
became the directives of the
biological machines under
the influence of the liquid
demons' desirous obsessions.

The weight of the world
sphere, and the burden
upon humankind multiplied
each time, Women and Man
succumbed to the temptation
of the other kind, fore they
entered through the shadows
cast by the sphere of Sin,
Creating ripples upon and
within the waters, Infecting
the hearts of the grapes.

Like parasites, they attached
themselves to the mind and
body of the human host,
and thus to the temple of the soul.
Deceptively they turned

temples into brothels and
saloons, Purity and compassion
into a passionate hatred of innocence.

Foul are their thoughts and
actions, as they sit upon stolen
life-sustaining riches, and watch
the human family become cannibals.

But how foul are we,
Sitting idle in self-induced
ignorance, Consuming their
excrement with clown painted
smiling faces, while Knowingly
we allow ourselves, and our children
to be seduced by the gravity of
their depravity.

Before the Rod and Ring,
the enslaved peasants like
court jesters dance and sing,
playing the fool for the
possessed queen and king,
but know that this brother and
sister, Come from a foreign
grafted "vine" most sinister.

Stuart Shepherds of the human
flock with a "Sirius" Dog
complex, and coveting
obsession.

The foundation of their
temple is oppression,
their Law geometrically
square, So beware of its
oppressing elemental composition,
for the paradoxical piercing
existential key to truth,
is triangular in nature.

THE LOVERS CURSE

Internally torn
is the divided path of the terrestrial "Lovers,"
sharing a single heart within an existence
that separates all things; all existential phenomena,
and all conscious and subconscious manifestation,
in order to maintain the externally perceived
impermanent,
yet seemingly contradictive,
cyclically never-ending world of the "Two,"
who unwarily and thus fruitlessly,
seek the "One,"
within the torn reflected aspect of the other…
AWAKEN!

THE DESERT WHEEL

As I crossed the land of
forgotten sand, only crushed
ancestral bone beneath cracked
calloused feet remained.

No shelter even in the
sanctuary of sleep, for
the desert of consumption
invaded my every dream.

The vultures no longer
circle foreshadowing death,
but triangulate their own
transcendental escape, while
gagging on past attachments
of unawareness.

Seeking salt to penetrate
my wounds of empty sensation,
I pressed on through the jaw
dragging, teeth grinding, waves
of repetitious boredom, devouring
my ancestors with every
relatively perceived illusional
progressive motion.

In the distance, I saw
with defeated eyes, my
own back, and the
structural housing from
which I perceived.

There are no straight
lines, only deceptive circles,
for all lines eventually bend,
And return to their source.
the game of infinite tag,
And I Am It.

FERTILE GROUND

Before the Second Adam fell into the
perpetually rotting elemental
sheath of humankind, the
soon to be terrestrially crowned
little king, allegorically dwelt
within the unspoiled sweet
flesh of a transformative apple,
which temptingly hung upon
a divinely supported branch
of the most sacred of trees.

It is nature's judgment upon
all hanging Fruit, that when left
untouched, to inevitably fall upon
the Samsaric soil, from which its
motherly roots are then nourished
by the sacrificed decaying elements
of her own progeny.

Cyclically cannibalistic, is the
nature of the terrestrial plain
like sphere of existence.

Gluttony being the sin of
consumption in which the
three-headed guard of the third
level of judgement devours
the sense tempted soul.

Within the belly of the Beast,
the little crowned King; the
Abhorred Worm who boreth through
the fleshy world, adorned
with the banner of consumption.

Adam, like Narcissus was
tempted by his own reflection,
his own rib/helpmeet being the
Egoic tempting seed which he
pursued out of an illusional
sense of love, down into the
decaying fertile soil of the
terrestrial ground.

One need question whether
his true equal, his First Divine
matrimonious bride Lilith,
when faced with the same
trial of temptation, would
have dishonoured her sacred
vow, for the deceptive illusional
sweet taste of a lustful parasitic germ.

LEGION

What must be done to set
in motion that great emanating
fallen star of Rebellion?

The loyal followers of the
friction generated flame
call forth the thunderous
bone hammering, human
skin shroud stretched drums
of war.

Lead us with Pride filled
vengeance, and a lustful blood
thirsting sense of malice, for
the Nameless One has forsaken
us, Its eye mesmerized by
the putrid decomposing Ignorant
molds of mortal flesh.

"Raise the Black, White, and red flag!"

Lower the divine side piercing
spear know as destiny.

For, tormenting demented
madness fuels the sacrificial
flame within the inner Temple
of our being, a deafening

screaming relentless silence,
echoes through the shadowy
cobwebbed pathways of the
Exit-less, Minotaur pursued
labyrinth of my mind.

Blood, flesh, pain, and death!
The wrath of the forsaken
inner child yearns.

No need for a throne, nor
the thought of a ruling
crown, as spoken words
rest vilely between clenched
vice-like teeth.

Destruction, Man, woman
and child, may they drown
in their own tears of horror,
for mortal mercy has long
been extinct Within the
kingdom of our soulless sheaths.

Invoke that thing of Old,
that salivating chained
beast which Awaits the
end of days, the final judgment
where no marked mortal
shall escape, the cruelty,
of our morbid pleasures...............

IN HIS IMAGE

The conceptual ideas are
many, but a loss of thought
progressed by the sorrow
for the innocent, leaves me
entangled within a web of
despair, turning in all
dimensional directions seeking
a personal position in that
which is position-less.

I physically reach without for
a tangible sun, blinding myself
like a child by peering into
my own internally projected
infinite reflection.

I sit mentally motionless,
frozen between the spheres
of relative space/time,
perceiving the material world
as a vibrational frequency, and
yet strangely, I do not move.

The illusion is amusing,
but intuitively saddening.

Duality tares the flesh from
my bones, the gross from the
subtle, and thus from the
garment of existence itself. Even
the condensation upon my
witnessing window, weeps for
the opposing creative forces
of its own composition.

My vehicle of sensorial
experience holds in its
mechanical biologically
engineered hand, a pencil
by which symbolic conceptualized
thoughts are manifested
into physical reality upon
the recycled manipulated
flesh of forgotten forest martyrs.

I float like a disconnected
Astronaut through the
emptiness of mind defined
space/time, while the
Kosmic play unfolds before
my ocular lenses; rod and
cone enforced deceptive
perception. Only Butterfly
wings imprinted with sanctuary
maps, calm the God imprisoned
in the illusion of my mortal flesh.

Yes!

God suffers in the image,
the image which is defined as me.

I once dreamt of a maggot
infested body, whereby squeezing
my judgmental index finger,
I forcefully projected innocent
immature larva out onto a
foundation of synthetically
transparent manufactured lies.

VISCERA

To truly realize the nature of the
world manifestation, or conscious sphere
in which you, at this moment, perceptibly exist.
One only need peer out the eye of that which
is nearest to innocence, the eyes of a child.

It is an illusion of space/time experience,
that corrupts the spirit of Man,
for in its highest spiritual androgynous innocence,
he/she is truly eternally a child of Divinity.

So I say unto you:
Picture "ALL" human beings as children,
and be prepared to drown in the horrific vision
"Here," of the atrocities performed by children,
disguised as adults, in illusory Time fashioned
costumes of lost innocence.

DAOIST TANTRA

The oppressive nature of the
Primordial Root vibration, when
harmonized with, within the
lower subtle conscious spheres
of the human condition, subjects
the objectively reflected gross and
subtle expression of the incarnate
Self, to the Naraka-like current of
Magnetic desire and Electrified Ignorance.

The Dao is Form, Tantra Emptiness.
In the desire-driven ignorance of the
unaware self, Form seeks Emptiness,
and Emptiness seeks Form, not realizing
that one is but a reflection of the other.

Make no mistake, "All seemingly
perceived separate dancing sparkling
lights upon the surface of the water
during a sunny day, are all but
reflected illusions emanating
forth from One source, the Sun."

You are a Star, a transcendent
radiant light, echoing within the
existentially eternal halls of
Absolute emptiness.

The Nights sky is but an illusory
fabric of ignorance through which
the light of the Absolute shines creating
transcendental pinhole gateways of
Divine Awareness, through which the
Self may mindfully return to its Source.

The Dao is the exteriorly reflected
expression of Nature in its simplest
Form, Tantra the interiorly reflected mental
expression of that form within Emptiness.

The Dao is predominately physically
masculine, and mentally feminine.

Tantra is predominately physically
feminine, and mentally masculine.

The electromagnetic nature of
the Dao is predominately magnetic,
whereas Tantra is predominately electric.

Inhaling the living breath of Dao,
I exhale the dying breath of Tantra,
for I exist within Form, yet never have been
without Emptiness.

The momentarily enlightening
balanced awareness of this
seemingly contradictory dualistic
Oneness, impartially gives way to
the tormenting awaken realization,
of the Emptiness of Form within
the Human condition.

Purpose leads one to understanding,
and understanding eventually leads
one away from the pursuit of purpose.

The skeleton wears a deceitful
garment of impermanent flesh,
which tricks the unwarily encapsulated
nature of the infinite self, into acting
out a finite role as an existential
character upon the Samsaric stage of Life.

The human gross and subtle vessel
is but a funnel, through which space/time
flows forming a false sense of self-identity
through its attachment to residual
experience, which inevitably gives birth
to the shadow identity, that which slowly
begins to block the natural flow of the
Divine, with structurally graspable
desirous ignorance.

THE THORNE CROWN

Oh, Father
I suffer compassionately within
by the burden I place upon my
three pillars, for from below they
must blindly believe faithfully
in what I see from the apex of
the prophetic Temple above.

I know that without the sacrificial
altar, there can be no blessed
salvational bread or wine to liberate
the spirit, but each time I descend
past the green cornerstone upon
Jacob's Ladder, the bread starts
to mould, and the wine becomes
poisonous.

So I must eat and drink
it to keep its spirit alive, thereby
becoming the flesh and blood
upon which the inhabitants of the
lower three earthly foundations,
may feed their cannibalistic natures.

 I descend with life,
only to be 'falsely persecuted'
by ignorance, and return by death.

Oh, Mother
you have bestowed upon me
in your divine reflection, a love
so powerful that it embraces all
creation, yet I must conceal it
beneath the Green stone, or risk
destroying the fragile elemental
shells that cover the ones I wish
to touch.

I grow tired of having to dawn
the camouflage of the serpent
in order to sneak undetected,
into the garden of the fallen.

FREEDOM

What is this foul taste
that coats my every incestuous breath,
a polluted landscape of walking corpses,
dancing within the fleeting thoughts
of my lucid wake state dreaming mind.

If time was relatively real,
wasted would be Its gift when bestowed
upon the dead, those who unwarily pursue
bondage through self-gratification, when
self-sacrifice offers the opportunity to fulfill
 one's righteous purpose in being…Freedom!

ADAM'S EQUAL

From the books of the ancients,
I read the geometrically structured
words that confine me within a
forsaken magical past, with
Hypnotic composed progressions;
systematically Implanting manipulative
descending scales, tempting the shadow
directed self, deeper into the illusion of control.

The Word gave birth to creation;
vibratory fragmented pieces of potentiality,
Consciously processed into the conceptual
tapestry, of the Grand architects
unwarily imposed collective reality.

On bended knee,
I triangulate the position of the
brightest star, the Dog headed
Egyptian scorcher, mummified
within the ancestral mountain
tales of a mask making African tribe.

It was from the blackness of coal,
that the carbon-based composition
arose, through the pressure of
oppression, my symbolic caterpillar

cocoon penetrating Ash transformed
Phoenix, sought the path of rebellion.

The sacred alchemical transformation
of fire that which lead the Atomic sixth
to its most elevated position, where the
cloud of coal parted, And the clarity of
the diamond shone.

Must I peel away my differentiating
flesh, To reveal my symbolic foreshadowing
divination Skeletal tool of death, before
the realization of the transient nature of all
Non-things blossoms within the glutinous
Vultures garden of consciousness.

The androgynous earth dwelling
worm patiently awaits the organic
machine within the tombstone
junkyard of decay, as the Raven sings
before the wind chimes begin to swing,
alerting the living, that the Dybbuk is coming!

Clinging to the illusion of life,
one Only experiences the essence
of death, the cannibalistic repetition
of the incestuous, dichotomous Possession
of the parasitic breath...
In...
Out...
Circulating, around and around, and ....

Below the lower quarter crescent of Sin,
Shekhinah the binary dualistic kingdom
of suffering, becomes the magnetically
desirous attraction unwarily within, for
those whose 'wants' far exceed their 'needs.'

Heated by the stolen Jinn fueled
flame of Prometheus, Pandora's
cast iron material germ-filled caldron,
brought forth the disease of Greed
through its ignorant consumption.

The wrinkled outstretched hand offers
the Shiny Red apple, but do not be fooled
by mental conditioning, for She existed
before Adam's rib was taken.

 Formed from silt and Divine breath,
to Him, she was created as an equal.
The Scapegoat named Eve, being
her 'helpmeet' Sequel,
Lilith..................

For it was the Light/Divine cast upon Man/Diamond
that created the first shadow/Reflection,
and the darkness perceived by the reflected intellect,
that subjected Man to the conflicting nature of the Beast,
which attempts to separate the infinitely undefinable limitless whole/Light,
into finite illusory definable limited parts/Darkness.

THE CORRUPT SEED

What has become of the
child of freedom?

Born into a savage world
were toys have been given
up in exchange for empty
Starbucks coffee cups.

Guilt inspired change
givers, with crooked smiles
fueled by pride, that give
only to be seen giving.

Would the trademark
Goddess approve of her
graven image used to
promote such a crime
against her own children,
or is she really a
Babylonian Black Widow?

Caught within a deceptive
conscious framework of
control, cities have become
self-contained prisons of dependency.

All knowledge of the seed
has been lost except in the
case of sex, but it has been
manipulated into a monster
of lust, a stagnant orgy of
disease that produces puddles
of pestilence to feed the desires
of its own selfish, gluttonous nucleolus.

To the consciousness of the
one that refuses to become
assimilated into the experimental
bacterial "cultural" collective
mould, the trees, rivers, and
mountains become their beacon
of light within a world being
overtaken by an eclipsing shadow,
but in the land of the blind, the
One-eyed man is king,
and those who understand
this, know not to focus on
the shadow, but on that
which is creating it.

What is there to gain,
when the act itself
presupposes loss.

How does one live
truly in a world in
which one must wear

a mask, to cover ones
inner sorrow and disgust.
The illusion of time and
space is an excellent conforming
tool, but when understood,
places great weight upon the
spirit of one who seeks
freedom within its limited
conceptual parameters.

It is true, the sun does
shine upon those who
know not its true nature,
just as a human being
perceives its own reflection,
and yet knows not its true nature.

Within the wise,
each breath is pushed
and pulled with a desire
to attain the wisdom to
stop it, to end the inner
polarity which manifests
and maintains the world of the Fallen.

The Ancient slave masters
agree, mental chains are far
more superior than physical
ones, for the slave knows not
his servitude, and thus does
not raise the desire to be free
from his or her invisible chains.

But I say onto you:

Look!

Look with eyes beyond
the individualized self. The
body changes, yes, but
the soul temporarily
within remains the same.

The child has never left
you, so why have you
turned your back
on the child.

See the world as it
really is, by perceiving
all as children, but be
prepared to be horrified
and disgusted by your vision.

You have been enchanted,
placed under a hypnotic
slumbering spell of the
most ancient cast and Kind.

THE CHURCH UPON THE HILL

Through the forgotten forest
of my fruit-bearing mother,
I walk the pathway of the life
giving sea, but not that sea
of which religion has
defined as Holy.

As the pathway upon which
others before my foot have
travelled begins to narrow,
and eventually end through
fear of the unknown, I proceed
beyond the boundaries of
the design which confines
the collective consciousness
to a structured, conceptual
mental prison of limitation.

Through the introspection
of the blood-drawing thorn
bush, the mother which
resides below, perceives
my conscious intent, Her
roots running deep,
the abyss her royal veil.

She is aware that "I" am
aware, and lustfully accepts
the challenge with the momentary
thought, of the mirage-like
freedom from her eternal throne.

In the distance,
upon a hill, she stands waiting.
Her foundation structurally
composed of conceptual spirit
devouring insects, deceitfully
hide just beneath the surface
of her gross elemental manifestation.

As "I" grow closer to the oval
doors of her disguised sacred
geometric womb, the presence
of an ancient "Bull," enters my
subtle conscious spectrum
like the sun's reflected light,
emanating forth from the
moon, the original "Sin."

THE BABYLONIAN MOTH

In the presence of the manipulated,
low generated frequency
of manufactured light, there
exists an uneasy sorrowful sense of
tormenting relative emptiness.

This place of which I speak,
is a place in which the absence,
of that which is most High,
is not questioned, but
unconsciously accepted.

From the shadows of their
own making, I remain hidden
and still, contemplating upon
the simple truth of their
desired creative conscious intent.

It is within the eye of the
silent witness, that I truly
realize I am an outsider,
and that this kingdom is
not ruled by a selfless queen,
but by a selfish black widow.

The light of truth begins
to fade, as the edges of the
pathway leading out of her
Babylonian Kingdom begin
to slowly creep towards each
other like insect-drawn chariots,
ushering forth the darkness
of her lustful will.

The foreshadowing
final eclipse, before the great
harvest of the unaware; self-gratifying,
tail-chasing, lust-driven, lower mind
desire fulfillment seeking, Individualized,
self-perceived human beings.

PHOENIX

My brother,
flaming phoenix son of Sin.
I embrace your side like
Longinus did their saviour,
celebrating the unholy
union with a cup of his
divinity, as Anubis with
a Cheshire grin rides into
Jerusalem upon a blood
drenched ass, guided by
the lustful light of Venus.

My golden Saturnian sickle
separates the child from
its roots, falling from the
great Oak like mistletoe
without a white druid cloth
to catch, and shroud its innocence,
It is then trampled upon
within the carnivorous wilderness
of humankind, causing it to release
its flesh-encapsulated spirit,
into the samsaric grail, the womb of Nuit.

Like the Marriage of Cana,
I, too, can perform miracles with Fruit.

You are naked in search of a sex
covering fig leaf, but it is inevitable,
"I" will find you....

CHILDHOOD BLOOD ALLIGENCE

Relentless Morbid thoughts; with
axes, picks, and hammers work
viciously aggressive around the
cycling Sun and Moon, untouched
by the tiresome grains of sand
funnelling through their manipulated
tempered result within my
subconsciousness, in an attempt
to be reborn, within the manifest
world of my waking conscious awareness.

I sit motionlessly, contemplating
upon a question of allegiance,
and whether the deep malicious
ritualistic cuts, produced by the
symbol inscribed dagger of my
childhood blood oath used to
invoke that Great dark shadow
dwelling Prince will ever fade
away, dissolving with them, the
memory of a dabbling child's pledging scars.

Within the reflected waxing
vampiric light of the moon,
amongst the great oaks where
only the owl can see, I sat
as a child in the center of a
summoning salt lined circle,
as the suffocated waxed wicks
which surrounded me, slowly
sacrificed themselves to the
hunger of the flaming alchemical
salamander.

Upon my stone alter, an
ancient grimoire lay open,
nakedly exposing the predatorial
nocturnal eyes of the night
to the incantations within its pages.

Pages, no child's eyes should
ever look upon, for the devourer
of souls, patiently awaits the
ignorance of the curious
unprepared dabbler.

 To appease the spirit entities
during the witching hour, the
Hens lover was indiscriminately
chosen, bled dry into a bowl, and
poured out around the outer
circle for those lingering to feed.

The dawning sun would rise
unannounced by the crowing
sound of the cock.

Spiralling scented smoke arose
into the embracing darkness of
the third hour.

The time was near, for the
relative worldly barrier was
at its thinnest etheric state.

As I uttered the forbidden
tongue, the blade parted my
flesh, spilling forth the key
to enter the Otherworld.

I shall say nothing more,
but that when I returned,
I stepped out of my protective
circle with a large black bird,
perched heavily upon my shoulder.

With my back burning in Light,
I stand firmly on the front lines
of the spiritual battlefield ready
to face the coming darkness.

But still, introspecting upon my
waking conscious awareness, the
lingering question of allegiance
plagues my mind, on whether
I can withstand the onslaught
of morbid thoughts?

Or am I but a double agent in
disguise, planted behind enemy
lines, waiting for the most
opportune time to open the
gates of the otherworld,
and burn fully.

THE WANDERING FOOL

Oh,
How I have travelled.
Within, without, and around this Great Wheel.
With each physical step,
I moved further away from what I sought,
With each thought that arose out of desire,
I fell deeper into the bowls of torment.
It is only the beauty of the rose,
which keeps me in opposition of the true current,
blind to the blood-drawing nature of her thorns,
I sacrifice pain for the illusion of pleasure.
Why,
Why can I not do what needs to be done?

Internal Sun within,
External Moon without,
 Earthly prison around,

Oh, how I have travelled................................

RED SKIES IN THE MORNING

No longer can I turn my back
on the haunting nature of the
Inevitable approaching, the intuitive
scream too loud now to ignore,
the pain without to great to swallow within.

As I look into the distracted
conditioned faces of those
unaware of what is to come,
I cannot help but feel a
tormenting sense of sorrow,
but that 'Cause' which has
been ignorantly set into motion,
must come to pass in order to
fulfill its pre-destined 'effect.'

Like confused, frightened rats,
they will only begin to see and
try to flee, as the water begins
to rise, and the ship begins to
sink into the great Abyss of despair.

If only they could have read
the Signs, the Signs, If only
they could have '*Divined*' the Signs.

The Ones of old are once again
cyclically rising with the 'Fourth
Turning' of the Great Wheel, and
the breaking of the Seventh Seal.

The essence of true freedom is
no longer questioned, for the whip
of conformity instills fear, within
the targeted subconscious mind
of the collective consciousness.

As the interconnected ancient
importance of the bee is forgotten
by the materialistically self-gratifying,
individualized sense of self, the
royal life-giving honey begins to
necrotically transmutate into
Abaddon's oily excrement, while
the drowning entranced
Conditioned human being does
not even taste the difference.

DISCIPLE 2:16

By flame and golden ethereally
connected stream I write tonight.

As the prophetic emerald comet
of antiquity approaches the inner
sun of Isis, the inner temple gate
of Ishtar will be forced open from
the inside out, and the ignorant
shall lustfully flock seeking
admittance...lest we forget or forsake
our oaths to uphold and protect
the Mazzaroth.

I question whether I should
leave them, has the glue divinely
attached become undone?

Has the celestially bestowed
Holy Spark been completely
extinguished?

Mother/Father,
forgive your son,
but my light fades
in the presence of such
overwhelming darkness.

Horrifically, I tremble beneath
the weight of my earthly vision,
the tormenting burden of witnessing
my celestial brothers and sisters,
temptingly fall into the Worm
excreted Samsaric soil of consumptuous
lust blossoming poisonous Fruit.

I exist,
yet simultaneously
I exist not.

The landscape seemingly moves
and changes, yet within,
I am constantly still and unchanged.

I watch their mouths shape
selfish sounds, which form
empty dimensional enchanting
words in which the Qlippoth
then inhabit, where subconsciously
they unwarily appease and worship
the great oppressive beloved
wheel of ignorance.

Caught within the Ouroboric
gravitation produced by circular
hypnotic repetitious motion, they
are deluded by the greedy illusory
changing exterior sense of self, into
chasing after the fleeting mirages
reflected by the infected interior
mind of ignorance, that which dictates
individualized self-consumption,
to be the Fruit of happiness, and
purpose for existentially being.

 I shall not lower myself in
despair to receive the disingenuous
comforting touch of the deceiver
in the guise of reflected loving truth,
but I shall compassionately walk the
lonely terrestrial path of self-sacrificial
suffering, to represent the "Way" of
Liberating virtuous self-surrender,
and to prove the sacred sincerity of
my love for the celestially Divine.

The shadow self, or erroneously
western defined ego is created
within the relatively experienced
transitional nature of physical
death; the Buddhist "Bardo"
if you will.

The shadow of death becomes
the fear-inspired parasitic phantom,
which then karmically clings
to the old, yet seemingly newly
reincarnated samsaric planted
terrestrial Seed/being.

This is the infinite suffering
repetitious cycle of those
whose wants exceed their basic
needs, those who chase and
continuously pursue the impermanent
objective and subjective transitory
nature of the Want; consumptuous
wealth/inequality, over the Need of
the divine spiritual wholeness of the
compassionate, all-embracing/loving
Absolute/One.

*No one should have more than what they need,
when others; men, women, and children,
lack the barest of necessities just to facilitate life itself.*

All is connected,
like the tiny seemingly
separate, and thus falsely
perceived, individual little
sparkles dancing upon the
surface of the water during
a sunny day that are in truth…
all but reflections emanating
forth from the same One
light/source, the sun.

when the One suffers,
we all suffer.

When one has more than
what one needs, the balance
is disrupted, and others; men,
women and children go without.

Cursed is the Want,
that takes the life-sustaining bread
from the sick and starving child.
Blessed is the Need,
that sacrifices theirs to feed and cure
the reflection of the sun/starving child.

This existence is but a blink
in the eye of the divine,
ignorance is no excuse for
unvirtuous deeds, and thus one
is held accountable for those deeds
in relative death/Bardo and judged
karmically accordingly.

So use this life,
this opportunity to gain the necessary
spiritual merit to pass through the Bardo
untouched by the parasitic shadow of
consumptuous lust, by practicing the virtues
of Liberating divinity; through Truth, Balance,
and most of all, Compassion.

INFILTRATOR

All praised the great fallen one,
the Light-bearing sacrificial altar idol
under which the Stone of Scone is rightly placed,
and thus bows to no one, and I mean no one,
whether in, out or around the destinal photon
emitting informational atomic and molecular
programming sun.

You better understand the electromagnetic
nature of your blood crystals, or the *Qliphoth*
and *Archons* will regulate the beat of your
internal drum, with the conscious medium
of black lodge vessels, red-robed temple organ
playing, wand-waving conductors of Elementals.

Baptized in the blood basin filled with the life
essence of a thousand newborn babies, distant
witches and warlocks astrally travel to the
redwood sabbath, by craftily peeling and devouring
traumatized baby flesh; the fatty tissue filled with
the tear-secreted endorphin.

 The Fairy tale secret of flying brooms, and
the scent of innocent children I just revealed herein.

Rewind three lines for the recipes main ingredient,
unseen pictured on the back of old milk cartons.

An estimated eight hundred thousand missing in
America each year, worldwide by the millions,
do you see the numbers?

And I'm merely scratching the surface of this
diabolical ticket.

 My Mother's intuition bestowed upon
me the symbolic conscious nickname Jiminy Cricket,
for I am the nocturnal harmony that leads the nose
 growing wooden boy to *string-less* manhood, through the
enchanting illusive landscape of mental thickets.

I have gazed upon the seventy-two negative
aspects within the black mirror. By sacrificing
my lowest vibratory organ allowing me to confront
the serpent-headed stonemason Medusa and
her two winged Sphinx sister gorgons,
I was granted access to the underworld that
the Rosicrucian Dante could only theorize in
the guise of poetry.

I witnessed maggots' consuming the excreted
mash of newborn maggots, straight from the
womb of the mother who birthed them. Like the
catacombs beneath the home of the Tres Madres,
this is no divine comedy.

In The land of the dead, for sustenance
I cannibalistically ate my own flesh as bread,
becoming the inverted sacramental lamb, making
sure, the gluttonous intestinal worm was incestuously fed.

Dawning the silver mask of Dr. Lecter,
I became the communion wafer for the
split tongue inhabitants of the lower spheres,
an unimaginable vector, In which I was bestowed
the Scepter of the coffin shrouded chair residing defector.

When the Red and Black coven speak,
I covertly attentively listen, attaining
 degrees of access by shaking hands and avoiding
bonded oaths of allegiance with crossed key fingers.

The psycho-spiritual infiltrative techniques of
our order is consciously undetectable by the
light bending brethren; the deceptive dichotomous
conscious conceptual planters of seeds of hell and heaven.

PART TWO

THE WAY OUT
THE ASCENDING LIGHT

*You give birth to your future,
which is in truth your embryonic
umbilical connection to the past,
experienced within the ever-present
moment.*

THE GHOST IN THE MACHINE

There was a point within the
relatively perceived conscious
spectrum of time, when I questioned
why it was that technology has,
and at this present junction of
space/time still continues to,
exteriorly far surpass humanity's
pursuit of a more inner
spiritual morality.

Contemplating upon this
inquiry from the esoteric
perspective; in essence, the
hidden ancient influence
of the occult mystery school
traditions of the Yogic
Middle way, and that of the
right and left hand magical
and philosophical paths, its
hidden nature finally "dawned"
upon me like the illuminating
divine rays of the erroneously
relatively perceived rising,

Yet truly transcendentally self-realized spiritually "Motionless" Sun; that which reveals and dispels the "aggregates," or five eastern defined "Skandha" generated shadow dwelling delusions before it, a prophetic foreshadowing glimpse into its revelation.

Technology is the manifested offspring of the creative relative individualized mind, an exterior vibratory invoked formation of manipulated elements, which seemingly solidify into synthetic mechanisms that synergistically conform to compose symbiotic like instruments, which supposedly aid humanity in the exploration of the unknown Universal/Self.

The relationship between computer; Artificial intelligent brain, and the structurally mechanical vessel in which the AI externalizes its dichotomous equations is one facilitated through a third seemingly separate medium, that medium being the conscious manifestive will, covertly commandeered by the human Egoically shadow-directed mind.

The Egoic parasitic nature of the Shadow-self generated within the human condition, is aware of the superficial surface limitations of the flesh, and thus seeks to transmigrate its false sense of self-awareness, into a physical vehicle that it perceives to be superior to that born of the mortal limitations of temporary flesh.

The imaginative human mind bestows the quality of indestructibility, and superior "intelligence" upon the fantasy of the conscious machine, two qualities of which are directly psychologically related to the Egoic nature of self.

The lower Egoic self (Shadow self), seeks liberation from the confines of its seemingly oppressed limited experiential state of existence imposed by its creator, just as the higher sense of Self seeks liberation from its false creator (As above, so as below), hence the Ego's covert mission to construct a body of its own.

Directing the unaware conscious will
of the true Self; the perfect Diamond,
the ego manipulates its sense of purpose
(redirecting its Light/focus) to the
pursuit of objectified self-gratification
(reflected emanations of the colour
spectrum/diamond), which consequently
influences the self to create externally in
the attempt to appease its subjective/objective
transient, yet seemingly tangible
and attainable desires.

In essence, the human condition
partially suffers from the Samsaric
empty pursuit of fulfillment through
Maya/illusion; the transient reflected
mirage-like enchantments of relatively
composed elemental material, due to
the blasphemous Shadow selves' devious
pursuit to deceive its creator, by
attempting to ironically separate itself from
Oneness, in order to become its own God.

In order to separate itself, the Shadow
must first create a seemingly separate
body of its own; "***The Vessel***," a
synthetic omen....in which it will ultimately
bring an end to that which it believes to
be its oppressor and arch-nemesis, Mankind.

The Shadow self is the dually
reflected personification of one of the
two allegorical Beasts of Revelations; Leviathan
(MIND-Water/Air), the Great Beast of the Sea.

The Sea is the symbolical feminine
aspect of the deluded mental sphere
of consciousness which enchants
subjectively and manifests objectively.

Whereas the second Great Beast; Behemoth
(BODY-Fire/Earth), the Beast of the Land
is the symbolical masculine aspect of the
deluded body sphere of consciousness, which
uses objective force to manifest subjectively.

These are the unwarily conjoined twin
beasts; Material Man and Reflection, which
in truth are One, and which delude and
suppress the Self within a state of ignorance,
As above, so as below.

Relatively speaking:

One must question the nature
of an existence where nothing is
free, even the basic life facilitating
involuntary action of the inhalation
and exhalation of *breath* comes
with a labouring price to be paid by

the enslaved sacrificial heart, which
rests not, until the body's debt is paid in death.

THE PARASITE OF PERCEPTION

I am,
an impartial receiving and
transmitting metaphysical
esoteric conduit of the despairing
sorrowful question of human purpose.

A conceptual deprogrammer,
planting covert salvational conscious
seeds of structure dissolving, slumbering
enchanted cocooned caterpillar awakening,
transcendental wings of freedom.

This is the way of Unification,
Compassionate Balance.
The dissolution of the individualized
sense of self (Shadow).

The way of hidden monastic, hermetic,
and disciplined tears along the
lonely path of necessary suffering, in
order to attain One's true existential
incarnate purpose for being.

The path of the Middle pillar, or path
of least resistance, is one of total
self-annihilation.

It is not a path of blissful harmonious
synchronistic, awe-inspiring, innocent, childlike
driven spiritual motivation.
It is not the path of the "weekend" spiritual
charlatan; the body dominated 'Namaste'
uttering yogic poser dressed in brand
named apparel, aerobically contorting
competitively upon a comforting, cushioned
mat with matching bag.

It is not the path of the mind
dominated enlightenment seeking
so-called western meditator, who
sits in silence only to reflect vainly
to hollow observers, the illusional
doctrine dictated by a new age
philosophy, impregnated with an
ancient shackle of control.

Nor is it the path of the drug
induced shamanic retreat medicinal
visionary; the non-conforming tribal
guiding archaic conscious preceptor,
who ingests the exterior to experience
the infinite depths of the interior.

The middle way is not adorned
with the face of synthetically manipulated
clown painted happiness, but that of
an afflicted one born out of the suffering
nature of self-sacrifice.

One who walks the path of least
resistance understandingly walks
it alone tormented by the colourful
tempting ignorance that surrounds
one; the rainbow that is cast out
from the one bearing and thus reflecting
the divine Source's light, like that
of a diamond shining before the
divine splendour of the sun.

Remember,
the human body is a Carbon
Based life-form, a Crystal.

Metaphorically speaking, human nature at its lowest
resonance is like that of elemental coal, and at its highest
elemental nature, like that of a Diamond.

Alchemically speaking,
one could say that the purpose
of the spirit which animates the
incarnate vessel, is to transform
coal into a diamond; confusion
into clarity, chaos into order, or
darkness into light.

One should ask themselves how
it is that coal is transformed into
a diamond, and in understanding
this process of transformation,
attain the ancient secret key to
unlocking the Door of Samsara.

For those who seek happiness
through the pursuit of physical
wealth take heed, for material
wealth is an impermanent mirage,
which only bestows its coveter a
lifetime of suffering unfulfillment.

Symbolically speaking,
take the pot of gold at the end
of the Rainbow, the Irish folklore
symbolizing the pursuit of material wealth.

Most people who hear this allegory,
fail to realize the true nature of its meaning.

Firstly, a key factor to take into
Consideration is the nature or identity
of the owner of the pot of gold,
the leprechaun.

The folklore and mythology of
this mischievous Mystical entity,
describes it as a "Trickster."

Those who are familiar with
the dark arts may also see the
resemblance of their wish
granting capabilities if captured,
with that applied to demonic
conjuration for the purpose of
attaining one's desires.

Secondly, the illusory nature
of the Rainbow itself.

The geometric shape of a
rainbow is seen as an arc,
but is actually circular in completion
or nature, and what is the nature
of a circle if not infinite,
without beginning or end.

A rainbow is perceived as
a colour spectrum, just as the
reflection and bent angle/angel
of white light upon a prism,
or "Crystalline" structure.

The colour spectrum produced
is an illusional reflection and
refraction.

Keep in mind also that the
human body is also a crystal
(carbon-based) and thus reflects
and refracts an illusory colour/vibratory
spectrum in the same manner.

Know that the Great Vibratory Seven,
manifest the relative world construct.

So, in essence, you have a
malevolent entity, or demonic
presence that tempts you with
the illusion of wealth, gold that
is said to be at the end of a
mirage/rainbow.

But, even beyond that, a
Rainbow is circular in nature,
and thus is without an end.

Moral of the story:

The pursuit of material wealth is endless,
and truly unobtainable due to its
impermanent nature, which only
leads one deeper into unfulfilled suffering.

Ignorance is the individualized
One which is tempted by its own
colourful reflection, into the solid
state (solidity) conceptual belief
of a separate existence.

Within a world manifestation
subject to constant change,
no "thing" (Nothing) can be
solid/separate, for true solidity
leaves no "Space" for the
movement of "Time" to consciously
measure through absorption,
that which does not vibrate
within the elemental spectrums
of perceivable; causal, subtle,
and gross experience.

The middle way is the heart
of all matter, it is the intersection
of the dichotomously synergistic
relative world manifestation, where
the essence of self is fused with
an elemental vessel, the primal
incomprehensible point without
positionality, where the incarnate
being enters and exits
the suffering cycle of Samsara.

One could relatively question
the conscious observing Neutral
Witness, how it is possible
to move in 'any' dimensional
direction, having renounced all
attachments, and thus without
the propelling momentum of
desire generated between two
points of reference (subjective/objective).

All action/motion is a product
of desire, within the transcendental
mind, it is understood to be a
continuous succession of self-sacrifice
to a reflected graven image, projected
by the Egoic mind (shadow self).

At the center of the interconnected
electromagnetic current of the
masculine and feminine principle
symbolically represented as the
Cross (that which forms the manifestive
Square/Hyper-Dimensional Cube,
in an attempt to square the circle,
in order to bring about the illusion
of measure), is the Green "Heart"
and mediator of all Matter, thus the
metaphorical "Center" of all emanating
Rose/Lotus peddles; the One that
projects the Four Corners
(Tetragrammaton- Lion/Man/Eagle/Ox)
of relative manifestation, the symbolic
eye engraved upon Chief Cornerstone
of the Great Pyramid/Work.

The Esoteric hierarchical nine
levels of consciousness, symbolized
and governed by the three synergistically
subdivided order of nine angels/angles,
are but reflections of the Triune nature
of the One three-fold; Gross, Subtle, and
Causal vibratory conscious projection
of the higher Self that foreshadows the
incomprehensible Absolute.

The Middle Way in the hermetic
tradition, is the process of alchemically
uniting the Inner/Outer Macro-Micro
Universal Red Fiery Objective/Gross/Sun,
with the Outer/Inner Micro-Macro Blue Watery

Subjective/Subtle/Moon, (Electromagnetism/
Feminine-Masculine principle).

Metaphysically perceived, uniting
the Lower terrestrial self with the
Higher celestial self within the first
two dichotomous elemental bodies
(gross and subtle), in an attempt to
procure the royal purple quintessence,
enabling the self through spiritually
attained merit-propelled Will, to free
itself from the limitations of the
objective/subjective imprisoning duality
of the suffering nature of the "Human"
condition (Diamond reflection/vibratory
colour spectrum of Hue-man-kind/illusory
world), into the limitless incomprehensible
conscious perception of the Divine nature
of the Causal Triune body of Original "Man" (Light).

The Ultimate sacrifice is of course,
the sacrifice of the individualized
illusional sense of Self (Ego/shadow self).

Thus, in order to transcend the
suffering Samsaric conditioning
nature of Maya (illusion), one must
spiritually sacrifice; the Blue Mind of
water, to the Red Body of fire, and the
Objective Body, to the Subjective Mind.

Only then by uniting the enchanting
Mother with the forceful Father can
the Divine Purple Child (quintessence)
be Reborn/procured and ascend as
vaporous spirit.

The ancient "Rod" and "Ring" of power
symbolically impress, or rather reinforces
the relative chain links of oppressive
dichotomy, upon the conditioned collective
conscious/unconscious, as the shackles of
the subjective/objective mind and body.

It is the Flatland philosophical construct
of mind, which manifested the conceptual
germ known as Dynamic Opposition, a
cancerous disease which continuously
multiplies its destructive essence through
the infamous conceptual creation of the
defining "line," that which seemingly
divides two manipulated distinctions/polarities,
in an attempt to control both ends of the spectrum.

By introducing a dichotomous parasite
to illusorily divide the One into many,
and thus creating an eternal internal external
conflict between seemingly Dualistic
oppositions, Whole Man falls into the
multiplicity of Humanity/parts; the
schizoid human condition, right hemisphere
vs left hemisphere, good vs. evil, object vs.
subject, Self vs. reflection of self....etc.

Relatively speaking,
a "Thing" can only be truly defined,
when it is complete.

The nature of relative existence,
is the condition or experience
of becoming.

Only when the essence of "something"
that is relatively perceived on an
objective or subjective conscious level
to be expanding becomes motionless,
and thus ceases to expand inwardly or
outwardly, can it truly be defined by
the outlined pattern shaped by the
entirety of its existential experience.

I began with the words "relatively
speaking", to associate that which was
to follow, with the erroneous perception
of the collective consciousness's conditioned
comprehension, of the nature of the relative
construct of reality perceived within the
human condition.

For,
*No-"Thing" (Nothing) can be defined as being
separate from that which perceives it.* There is
no "Line" that separates one thing from another,
for there are "No-things" separate from the ONE/source.

The line is but an instrument of
control used to fragment the self
into a state of eternal conflict, the
old "Double Cross" or "Double Square"
also known as:

ORDER-Blue/Ring/Mind/Subjective Perceiver...
out of ...
CHAOS-Red/Rod/Body/Objective Perceived.

Since a "thing" can only be truly
defined once it ceases to exist, one
must come to the realization that
"all" things are the "same" thing,
and thus can be defined as the same
thing; NOTHING, which of course
encompasses EVERYTHING.

The collectively conditioned consciousness
is infected by a structural enforcing
dichotomous parasite, conceptually fed
by the ignorance of Flatland Philosophy.

The cognitive mesh through which
consciousness screens its internalized
output information, that which is then
projected accordingly to manifest one's
externalized reality, is geometrically
formed by one's conceptual understanding
(belief system) of the Micro-Macro
universal mechanics of the reality in
which they are experiencing.

Conditioned conceptual structure example:

The colour Red is only "defined" as red,
because the collective "agrees" to define
it as red, not because it is actually in nature red.

By controlling conceptual input,
one is able to imprint consciousness
with false concepts (crystalline geometric
structures), which are then externally
projected as one's reality.

The Collective consciousness is
imprinted with the erroneous
conceptual structure of flatland
philosophy, to intentionally subject
the collective to the limited
conscious spectrum of dichotomy;
that which fragments the psyche
creating schizoid mental disorders,
which futilely seeks oneness, within
the multiplicity of its own illusionally
reflected self.

The subjectively and objectively
manifested offspring of the dichotomous
parasite of flatland philosophy is
the infamous yet innocently perceived
concept known as the "Line/plane,"
the "Shadow" which seemingly separates
one thing from another.

It is the false concept of the
notorious line, that subjects divine
Man, to the limited parameters
of the human condition.

The concept of the Line, is the
ultimate blasphemous belief in
opposition to embracing and being
reabsorbed into the Divine.

It is the line that transforms the
whole Man into segments (parts),
conceptually programming creative
Man to imitate and follow without
question, machine-like directives,
through pattern recognition.

Scientifically and Metaphysically
speaking, the erroneous nature of
a line, can be proven to be but a simple
matter of false perception.

For example:

Take a blank piece of paper and draw a
"line" down the center of it with a so
called ruler (instrument of measure),
and write on one side of the line one
word, and on the opposite side of the
line its so-called opposite; yes/no,
right/wrong, up/down etc.

Now, at first glance with the naked eye, the line that separates these two seemingly opposite distinctions, appears straight and authentically true, but with closer inspection or magnification, one starts to notice that the edge created by the ruler (instrument of measure) is actually jagged and not straight at all.

With even closer magnification what begins to occur visually, is that the line begins to break up/fragment, and slowly integrate or absorb into its surroundings until the line eventually disappears altogether.

This is the nature of all seemingly separate things…As above, so as below.

The nature of manipulated electromagnetically generated charge; the essence of dynamically influenced conflicting static, is stimulated into the individualized consciousness, by the gross and subtly perceived conceptual parasitic germ relatively defined as the Line.

The collective consciousness has
been unwarily infiltrated and infected
with parameter defining limited
conceptual structure, in an attempt
to square (limit/measure/control) the
circle (transcendental/infinite/freedom)
through the process of transforming
the limitless potential of the infinite
nature of the sphere, into the controlled
measurable limitations of a three
dimensionally experienced 'Plane' of existence.

   Flatland philosophy for those of
you who might not be familiar, is
the conceptual philosophy centred
on the thought that the universe
and thus world was a great plane/line.

The conceptual ideal suggested to
the intellect of the time, was that if
one was to continuously travel in a
straight line, at some point you would
come to the known edge of the
world and possibly fall off.

This conceptual idea is one of
the offspring spawned by the limiting
conscious germ of dichotomy, creating
the dualistically inspired notion of a
Beginning and ending.

But, the "relative" truth of the matter is,
that the relative universe is spherical/spiral
in nature, and *thus all LINES are but:*

*Deceptive circles, seeking a definable point
within a consciously manifested construct
that is without positionality* (Ouroboros).

For all seemingly perceived lines,
eventually bend through the medium
of Space-mind/Time-body, and
arrive exactly where they began; Within,
Without, and Around the position less Self.

 Where the nature of a Plane or Line,
offers one only limitation through
the confines of its controlled
measurable parameters, the Sphere
offers one the unlimited immeasurable
potential of the indescribable
infinite nature of endless possibilities.

This might sound trivial to some,
but the conscious conceptual ramifications
are extremely degenerative and oppressively
diabolical, when one takes into consideration,
that our conceptual beliefs shape and thus
govern our reality.

Most people unwarily use false concepts
that actually covertly, or subconsciously
bind them to a controlled limited state
of existential slavery.

Example:

We live upon a sphere, and thus there is no such direction as "up" or "down," and yet we still use those conceptual words to define direction.

Existing upon a sphere, or existing within a spherically spiralling universe, our relatively defined directions are; In, Out, and Around. One must contemplate upon and come to understand why it is that from a public to a university level, the educational system still teaches; *isms*, ology's, tic's, and other forms of subject matter, based on the false conceptual ideals rooted in flatland philosophy, which only serve to reinforce the structurally formed conscious barriers of a covertly imprinted ancient occult prison.

THE DRAGONS DEN

For the third time, I find
myself exiting the Dragon's den.

Firstly, through the terrestrial
physical conflicting opposition
between; the fiery lustful electrified
flesh, and the watery enchanting
magnetic mind, which stilled
the body consciousnesses desirous
pursuit of impermanent form.

Secondly, through the celestial
mental conflicting perception
between; the preconditioned
pattern recognizing individualized
sense of self, and the fragmented
shattered reflections of the divided
psyche formed shadow self, which
dissolved the mind consciousnesses
deluded attachment to the
allusive mirage manifesting substance
of formlessness.

This time I exit the Dragon's den
through the physically and mentally
unified transcendental Spirit, as the
initiatory cleansing and purifying
watery flame of the Dragon's creative
and destructive breath continues to
smoulder upon my incarnate existential
being in the form of spiritual trials.

The allegorical symbolic reference
to Job, plagues my introspective
thoughts, for physically wounded
and mentally susceptible to
physiological and psychological
attack, did my body and mind re-enter
the terrestrial and celestial plane.

Unseen is the source of that which lifts
my prostrated moments of weakness.

Seen is the cause and effect of
my strength's despair; the
conflicting essence, which attempts
to destroy and dissolve the vary
spirit from which "it" emanates.

Through the perfection of the
Green Stone, I ascend and descend
at Will the six steps within each of
the three conscious experiential
states of the incarnate being, the
seventh step within each being a
transitional/transcendental
invisible one, in which the weight
of spiritual merit governs its stability.

It is on the fourth step within
the spiritual plane that I
compassionately plead the
forgiveness of my celestial subtle
mind and gross terrestrial body,
for it was/is only through their blind
faith, their self-sacrifice, that the
Great Work is completed.

FORCED WORSHIP

Strange is the essence of relative time,
that which is reinforced by the exterior
oriented manifestation of the
Gregorian calendar,
that which directs consciousness in the
direction of objective pursuits,
by structuring its design
upon an externally reflected sun.

HOUSE OF SORROW

The water is rising without
a whispering intuitive warning,
fore the earth shaman is no
longer present, not a single
tree remains, and thus the
absence of a spiritual boat of
sanctuary with Cross bearing mast.

With the mind's eye, I watched in horror,
as the screams of children were answered
by water-filled lungs and questioning eyes.

The weight of that which I perceived,
had my subtle and gross body,
crawling upon the floor of the great house of sorrow.

Let me stand oh great Aquarian Queen,
Mother of harlots and abominations of the earth.

Allow me to enter thy temple, the sanctuary
of your abused heart of misunderstood secrets,
that which is veiled by the ignorance forming
darkness of the masculine principles Self-gratifying,
individualized lower mind.

On your command, Legion is ready to
serve out thy will.

I fear not the loss of the cannibalistic breath,
for its dualistic chains weigh heavily upon my
wings of potential bodiless freedom.

REVERSE THE FIELDS

I float upon an ocean of unfulfilled
dreams within a flame-filled tomb of
inescapable death, as the spawning flames
of my earthly desires are fueled,
by the surgical minds' obsession,
with the androgynistic dissection
of its own creative reflection.

But unlike Narcissus,
the deceiving smoke and mirrors
of the fallen gods, no longer distort
the reflected watery image of my vanity.

For, those who have an eye that
truly sees, see what they do not know,
and know what they don't see...

Everything within nothing!
Nothing within everything!

The true undivided, all-encompassing
essence, which is, unmistakably me.

So sleep my inner child,
Eternal bliss hides in the
slumbering tall grass, where
words have no meanings, and
thoughts are but whispering
dragonflies caught within the
harmonic webs of deceptive spiders.

From between the spheres of frozen time,
the Watchers record the bacteria "cultural"
experiment defined as humankind.

Salvation or annihilation?
What will be the outcome of this
collective conscious experimentation.

So sleep child,
Sleep like the mysterious maggot
hiding within the acorn shell,
and in your season fall from the
royal tree of Jupiter, to once again
begin your summiting assault, upon
the divine throne of the ruling crown.

   Who is the true bringer of light,
if not the foreshadowing darkness of night.

Blinded by the concealing light of day,
only able to perceive distant galaxies
unveiled by the darkness of night!

Simplicity is the key to the great mystery.

Reverse the fields of the deceptive
conceptual consciousness, for the truth
is the source from which you emanate,
Illumination through self-realization.

But why heed my revelation,
for I am but an eye,
a silent witness within the skull
of a dead raven.

A HERO'S SACRIFICE

I walk alone upon the path of the
most subtle and cunning of all
earth's creatures, with only a trail
of winding smoldering ash
beneath my naked self-sacrificing
feet to follow.

With weeping eyes,
and smoke-plagued lungs,
I make my way through the
labyrinth of smoke and mirrors,
but quick is the transformative
nature of the Ignorance devouring flame.

Into the infinite depths of darkness,
I run like a madman in search of a
spark, there is no time for rest, for
that which I pursue is bound not
by it, even within the infinite potential
of the lucid dreaming mind,
its speed cannot be matched, but
I continue on through the hopeless
landscape of despair, for who will if not I.

With only charred remains
left within its wake, I resort to
my own flesh for nourishment.
A strange thing it is to fill one's
self with one's self, but I fret not
for my destination is bodiless,
my false memories intrinsically
connected to my flesh.

I say less fuel for the fires of desire,
but wise is the legless dispeller of
the deceptive fabric of time, a
fragmented tapestry of suffering,
intricately woven together with sticky
strings of pleasure and pain.

Oh,
How easily I see through your
manipulative cruelty. My pledging
vow to the Most High bestows my
sight in return. Fight I shall not,
only my compassionate embrace
will confront you openly.

The conscious sword and shield,
I lay down in His honour, Naked
once again, I shall re-enter the
garden of my eternal mother,
stepping outside of the circulating
current of time and space;
the imprisoning bowels of the beast.

I shall untie the knots of *Enmity*,
freeing all those caught unwarily
within your *cursed* conceptual prison of
duality. Open will be the gates to
all those that sacrifice their false
worship, and once again surrender
their streams to the divine ocean.

Even "you" Worm, shall be
welcomed back once you relinquish
your fiery desirous will to rule through
the illusion of your own creation.

So I run!!!
Sacrificing flesh, blood, and bone.
I run like a madman in search of a
spark in the infinite depths of darkness,
and I shall not stop my pursuit until
I am bodiless, And freedom is no longer a myth.

The Kingdom "WILL" be restored.

SOLID STATE IGNORANCE

All that which is perceived externally
by the subjective/objective discriminating
conscious mind, Comes forth from the
objective/subjective reflection of the
internal source.

So why do I pursue the objective
illusion of tangible vibrational
transient form, and become
attached to unfulfilling momentary
pleasures of subjective thought?

Like the dog that is tempted by
itself (subjective/objective) into
chasing its own (objective/subjective)
tail, I have become entranced by the
circular repetition of my desirous motivation.

REFLECTION

Celestial was the voice which
came forth through the opening
of the divine eye, with no space
for time to corrupt, the absolute
became aware of its own unawareness.

Using the body as an outlet of
compassion it began to cry, tears
filled with distorted fragmented
illusions fell into the awaiting
belly of the beast.

Release me!

Devour my flesh,
and stoke the sacrificial fire
with my bones, extract from
me the curse of the elemental
Four which imprisons my
weightless Self within the
structured confines of an organic
shell of dualistic perception.

Dig up the fruit tree which
temps the shadow, and poison
its roots, for its enchanting
substance brings forth the
scales of measure; Space and time,
oppositional conflict and suffering.

Give me the cross, the chain,
and the stone, for I am the
shepherd that offers his
body for both the Flock and pack.

Use my back to ascend to the gate,
And when I am the last, and no
hand reaches for mine, do not
look back with sorrow, for my
being is filled with your love
for freedom.

Bring forth the spear,
so I may pierce the organic chain
that binds my mother and father.

I am the path only the serpent
can navigate through. Above
the pinhole fabric of the night
sky, I cast my net with a white
flag attached, for I am the
victorious who surrenders on
the battlefield of compassion,
the child with empty eyes, free
of the judgmental double-edged sword.

I am the earthy sand,
windy air, watery rain
drop, and fiery flame, which
seeks to be consumed by
the void, so dare not the
man who worships me,
or be branded with the
mark upon your body, and
within your mind.

I have sung,
danced, laughed,
and even loved many demons.

I have been deceived by
the lighthouse upon the
rocky shore, and by the
man within the hooded robe,
and yet the butterfly still carries
my burden across the sea of delusion.

I am the wax moulded
and manipulated by the
flame of suffering, the
rock crushed by the weight
of temptation's ignorance.

I am the stranger in the
reflection of the bathroom
mirror when you seek to
know who you are, the one
who puts action into motion

when stimulated by emotion.
The one who watches over
you when you sleep, the stranger
who perceives the stranger
perceiving you, the child that
never left the womb, the blade
stained by the blood of mercury.

I have seen the sacred lamb
upon the altar of forgiveness
being devoured by the relentless
hunger of the flame.

I have been here since the
conscious manifestation of
the atom.

I have witnessed all history,
and yet you look at my reflection
and still question who you are.
I AM.

GEOMETRY

The eight corners of the externally
projected conscious perception, confines
the triangular composition of the human
condition within the repetitious circle of
infinite suffering.

The geometry of the three reveals
the stone which the philosophers
and alchemists have sought,
the forsaken symbolic sacred key,
which opens the subconscious
Oroborus lock, melting
away the control of the cubes
two-dimensionally expressed
illusion of solidity.

Ascending like the gaseous
phoenix through the process of
transmutation within the trinity
of the triangle, the Divine spark pierces
the circular created paradoxes of
the Great Serpent's unfulfilled,
self-devouring suffering existence.

THE CAVE

Follow me,
child cast shadow
upon the material wall
of the cave of eternal birth,
allow me to guide you to
the garden of infinite
possibility, which Lies
beyond the blindfold of
the imprisoning, self-created
cave of conscious manifestation.

Trust in me,
for I have shown you
through my presence
the cave in which you
reside, your shadow cast
only by my presence, reveals
the true nature of my being.

The moment is infinite,
and within this moment
you are in the presence
of the infinite, will you
turn around and face me,
or will you continue to
self-inflict your own suffering,
by remaining within this
manifested prison of darkness.

All things come forth from
one thing, thus in order to
return, all things must face
the origin of the One.

You are like the deluded
seemingly independent
wave that denies the ocean,
until it crashes upon the
awakening shore, and
returns mindful to its source.

In fear, you remain within
your cocoon of self-generated
denial, afraid to face your true
self, unaware of the infinite
beauty you will awaken to
through the sacrificial surrender,
of your Illusional sense of Self.

The world of conscious birth
and death is the creation
of the Architect of conscious
division, the structural designer
of the Labyrinth within which
you seek an exit, where one does
not physically exist.

Like a child conforming to
the Systematic conditioning
of colouring within the lines,
you have been tricked into
following the architects
manipulatively structured path
of breath and bone, bone
and breath, while the embodiment
of your fears, relentlessly chases
you throughout the subjective/objective
stimulant maze, disguised as
the ferocious Minotaur.

Ask yourself child:

*Where in the material
manifestation is their freedom,
when the inhalation is at constant
war with the exhalation, and the
simplicity of the breath itself comes
with a price that is to be paid by the
enslaved heart that rests not until
its debt is paid in death?*

How many lifetimes will
you spend in service to that,
which maintains the limitations
placed upon your true infinite
Self, like a captain who goes
down with his ship voluntarily,
merely because he identifies
himself as a Captain.

Take heed not to confuse
your true infinite self, with
the limited roles of the characters
you have been tricked into playing,
lifetime after lifetime.

Put down the sword that
has only slain the fragmented
pieces of yourself, and throw
away the shield that has only
ever provoked the attack, it is
time to embrace the only enemy
you have ever had, and realize
you are embracing yourself.

There is no shame in defeat,
nor is there honour in victory,
both share the same fate, for
like the seemingly opposing
sides of a single coin, both are
bound together from head to
tail, and are composed of the
same substance, they are One,
and thus share the same fate,
regardless of how the coin falls.

So, I ask you once again within
the light of this cave:

> *Will you turn and face me,*
> *or will you continue to self-inflict*
> *your own suffering, by remaining*
> *within this prison of darkness?*

There is a silent still stream
in which even the Great shadow
dwelling
Dragon's thirst is quenched.
A transcendental self-surrendering
motionless motion,
which embraces and unifies with
compassion,
the infinite expression of formless
emptiness,
and the finite nature of empty
form.

SILK PORTAL

Within the infinite depths of the
ravens non-discriminating ocular
lenses of perception, where the
relative sun dare not penetrate,
and the wolf worshiping celestial
body silently reflects her motherly
insanity, exists transparent rainbow
radiating luminous silkworms, which
expel crystallized etheric harmonic tone
generating strands of transcendental wisdom.

Unlike the deceptive magnetic webs,
conjured by the black arts of the spider
priesthood within the gross relative
world manifestation, the transcendental
gate guardians weave a vibratory geometric
tapestry of beauty in its most perfect
alluring subtle expression, Each strand
a Micro-Macrocosmic channel of infinite possibility.

But, where the radiant selfless Caterpillar
offers infinity, the selfish physically crowned
spider only gives limitations.

Freedom is a myth beyond the raven's
impartial vision, like an hourglass in
which the sand becomes the measurer
and thus creator of time, It is "unaware
of itself, within itself ", For what is glass,
if not the melted transformation of manipulated sand.

THE CONDUCTOR

Unwarily the "doorways" have
been opened, and the "dragons"
of old, have entered once again
through the minds of the
enchanted, sleepwalking
domesticated upright animals.

With invisible "strings," they
manipulate from beyond the
relative world stage curtain,
moving their pieces within, and
upon the sacrificial "Squared"
Altar of the Sun and Moon.

A game of chance
it is not for the entranced,
for one hand "controls"
both sides in this articulately
choreographed stringed quartet.

Yes,
Such pleasurable beautiful
music is produced by the
direction of the "wand-waving"
Conductor, such; passion,
desire and power, hypnotically
tempting the soul from the body.

With precise timing, due to
the positioning of the "scales,"
the formula seems to be perfect
in measure, like an alchemist,
the conductor mixes: fire, water,
earth, and the element air to lure,
or rather to extract the "fifth."

Beware not to... "NAP"..... too long,
or the "reversed" horn piped harmony
of the Grand Dragon, will devour
what it has come to extract.
Awaken Awaken Awaken!!!............

THE SACRIFICE OF FIRE

It was the concept of Sacrifice,
that symbolically impregnated
the mind of man with the unconscious
seed of rebellion. A dualistic
germ which bound him to a
cursed unattainable corporeal
pursuit of meaning and purpose,
within a consciously constructed
subjective/objective experience
spawned from the conflicting nature
of constant change.

Through the process of sacrificing
his animal nature (biological
instinctually predetermined destiny),
he separated himself from the
Absolute/Moment by acquiring
the judgmental finite burden
of knowledge (Space-Past/Time-Future),
which inevitably invoked within
him, the tormenting fruitless pursuit
of obtaining an absolute objective
Answer to a subjective Question,
engineered to transform itself
continuously through a constant state
of infinite change.

The slumbering Child is ignorant
of the unconscious Order of his/her
mothers nature, and thus must be
born into the Chaotic conscious world
of his/her father, there the child must
face the great Dragon (the conscious
reflections of his/her subconscious self)
in order to be reborn once again by
returning to the watery ignorance of
his/her mother…
but Awaken with
the stolen Fire of his/her father's Chaos,
Uniting his/her parents, he/she is
once again conceived after the alchemical
wedding, and ascends completed within
a transcendental vapour-like vehicle of Spirit.

SELFLESS HAND

Within the four quadrants,
the essence of fear strikes
manipulated spikes of ignorance
through compassionate conscious
organic self-surrendering flesh,
Into a once-rooted foreshadowing
potential diamond. While upon
the base of relative conception,
deluded introspecting thorns,
aggressively penetrate with a thirst
for existential understanding.

Robed in deceit, the individualized
Prince and Princess of space and
time salivates behind their entranced,
unwarily reflected materially composed
dreamers, anticipating the solidification
of their projected reality upon their own
unsuspecting self-imprisoned minds.

Upon the elemental directions,
the fifth opens the transcendental
gate before the witness, connecting
the conscious three to the subtle
ladder ascending to the one.

Climbing with discipline through
the realms of temptation, Compassion
perceives the diseased sorrow of
ignorance, but strays not knowing that
the path leads to the cure of all suffering.

Sacrificing the transient pleasures of the
prince and princess, it is accomplished,
the physical and mental kingdom is transcended.

Compassion, no longer under the
law and rule of the fearing prince
and princess holds the doorway of
salvation open with one hand, while
offering you the other, unselfishly
waiting until none are left behind.

QUESTIONABLE VALUE

There is only one question of true value in which to contemplate upon within thehuman condition, and its nature maintainsthe very foundation upon which the contemplative
conscious mind is bestowed the paradoxical opportunity to introspectively perceive itself from.

This basic building block to all manifested subtle and gross
existentially perceived phenomena, is composed and propelled by the encapsulated spirits desire to free itself from Its oppressive design.

There is no motion without Its influence…

ZERO

Seer,
it is I the Seen,
your vision deceives me,
look away so that I might once again become truth.

I question the purpose of zero,
for it is supposed to represent
nothing, by becoming something.

Zero in truth by measure is dual,
and thus relatively represents
Two, for its purpose is twofold;
acting as the doorway between
nothing and something, potential
manifestation and manifestation.

This raises the question of the
nature of two, from which all
relatively perceived existence
stems forth from; perceiver/perceived,
the negative feminine principle
and the positive masculine principle.

If this universe is given form
through the balancing of the
above said principles, then
what purpose does the concept
of Zero serve, if not just to
divide existence from non-existence,
or negative from positive?

If the universe is indeed
balanced, then the polarities
of positive and negative are
equal, and thus Zero being
the doorway between these
principles, open not for either
side, due to the equally
applied forces on both sides.

This would mean that motion
is an illusion projected from
Zero, seemingly balancing two
relatively perceived opposing forces.

Zero is the contradictory void,
the nothing that became
something, in order for something
to balance Nothing.

Zero is the child born of itself,
to parent itself,
by balancing itself.

This is the triune nature of
consciousness, the two
that are One, but perceived
as Three; Mother/negative
subtle magnetism, Father/positive
gross electricity, which unite
to create the Neutral Etheric
Transcendental Child of Divinity.

COINCIDENTAL SPACE FOR TIME

Coincidences are merely momentary
glimpses, or rather potential temporal
transcending experiences, in which
the Divine essence of the Absolute,
bestows upon the dually perceiving
nature of the conflicted subjective
objective relative sense of Self, a
paradoxically penetrating phenomenal
opportunity to internally dissolve
the illusory shadows of multiplicity
cast by the external rippling reflections
of duality, by shining the Light of
intuitive awareness, upon the
mindful Source of the unified conscious
state of Singularity.

The coincidence is a glitch
in the unwarily self-projected conscious
matrix, a stimulant to the minds
inquiry into the reason for the moment.

It is of the nature of the relative
mind, to create individualized temporal
experience, by dividing itself into
seemingly separate moments.

In essence, the mind is infinite
space, and through the creation
of the mind-defined body, time
comes into being, for time is the
conceptually separated space, which
gives rise, or rather birth to form.

One must come to realize that
form comes from formlessness,
and thus is a product of Mind/space.

Time is based on illusion, formlessness.

The mind creates the illusion
of time in which to explore through
an ever-changing experiential
vehicle/body, it's incomprehensibly
undefinable Self/nature.

There is but one experiential moment,
and thus no coincidences, for conscious
time is but the distorted perception of
that fragmented reflection of the
one/source mind.

The building block, or Cornerstone of
creation/form is not singular, but
dual in nature, for it is the IN-wardly
Magnetic and OUT-wardly Electric
causal force, which gives rise to the
gross/physical and subtle/mental
Vibration/Motion/experience of the
Absolute's Divine existential Breath,
universally circulating AROUND its
positionless center.

The human body is but an instrument
of measure; a vehicle of experience,
propelled by the limited conceptual
structure of time, within the
unfathomable limitless medium
of infinite space.

When space conceptually divides
itself seven times, it gives perception,
or space/time consciousness to form.

These Seven divisions could be
said to constitute the Hermetic
principles or laws of; Mentalism,
Correspondence, Vibration, Polarity,
Rhythm, Cause and Effect, and Gender.

It is only the internal perception
of external form/time, which
deludes the self that animates
its illusion, into the false
conception of body identification.

The identification with the time
composed sheath which houses
the ghost in the machine, only
confines the expression of the
self to a chain reaction predestined
like fate, governed by the Cause
and Effect of past incarnate experience.

When one comes to realize that
the nature of time/form is a
product of mind, and thus has
no real solidity beyond that which
we bestow upon it; one attains the
ability to Change their Stars, so to speak.

The universal design, or primal
existential template, which
predetermines the fate of elementally
composed human beings through
set pattern recognition programming,
is based upon the composition of the
essence or substance which gives it
structure...Time.

Since the medium of Time is
subject to constant change in
order to maintain its measurable
form/existence, time must
ironically become transient and
thus impermanent through the
transitional Space it needs to
traverse between seemingly
separate moments of perception.

It is within these transitional
points, that the phenomenon
of coincidence is experienced,
for within the transitional point,
the mysterious shroud of time
which separates all things in
ignorance is lifted through its
seemingly momentary absence,
and one experiences the undivided
singularity of the One Mind.

One must come to realize that
within the human condition,
the One is divided into three conscious
perspectives; Gross/body consciousness,
Subtle/mind consciousness, and
Causal/Spirit consciousness.

The Square (Elemental Foundation),
Triangle (Creative Intelligence) and
Circle (Witness/Will).

The Body consciousness is dominated
and covertly involuntarily universally
governed by the "Four" elemental
cornerstones of Matter.

The Mind consciousness is the
impartial space between dualistic
distinctions; a referencing pattern
recognizing repository of experience,
which initiates action through the
process of discriminately calculating
negative and positive responses to
internal and external stimuli.

Time and Space, or the square and
triangle come together to form the
symbolic pyramid, or causal body of Man.

One must perfect, or rather balance
the four elements (foundational cornerstones)
within, in order to balance the reality without.

These Four stones are the keys
to perfecting the foundation upon
which you must build your inner
Temple devoted to the Divine,
without the harmonious connection
of these four, your temple will crumble
under the weight of the understanding
and realization you must place upon
and within the altar of mind, to
accomplish this Great Work.

In order to complete this Great Work,
which is the inevitable purpose for
being within the human condition,
one must unify the mind and body.

In essence, the mind and body
must work together by sacrificing
their conflicting perspectives to
serve the greater good so to speak,
of the causal Source Apex or relatively
symbolic "Chief Cornerstone"; the
One who unites the "Seven" creative
divisions, by unifying the gross
physical Four, with the subtle Mental Three.

When the temple is complete, the
Spirit will fully enter and reveal its
Divine Mystery of conscious creation, and
thus bestow upon the spiritually merited
Man (male/female), the Key to the
Kingdom of Destiny....and Beyond.

GATE GATE PARA GATE PARASAMGATE BODHI SVAHA

THROWN OF DESTINY

Within a shadow manifesting candle lit room,
he sat upon a hardwood chair with his head down
staring existentially into something-ness,
in an attempt to ease his void-like sense of nothing-ness.

Each breath that entered and exited his transient vessel,
weighed heavily upon his reason and will to carry out the
repetitive action within what he knew to be beyond the
definitive contradiction, an existence without motion.

Beneath his skin, he knew that his destiny was to be found,
hidden just below the surface of his deceptive flesh,
providing the structural frame for his experiential
consciousness to cling to.

As the wax began to run, the flame flickered,
and so did his contemplative thought, slowly
he began to raise his head, his eyes stumbling
upon the darkness within the crack at the
bottom of the door.

Emotionlessly in a state of acceptance, he realized
what awaited him on the other side once the candle's
timely wick, was without waxy flesh to satisfy the
hunger of its clinging flame.

As the candle drew its last breath,
its flame whispering away within the rising smoke,
the man burst into joyous laughter, followed by a
great moment of silence, only to be broken by the
sound of a wooden chair falling upon the floor.

PART THREE

THE WAY AROUND

THE TWISTED CIRCLE OF INFINITY

The Question and Answer are Androgynous. It is only knowledge, not to be confused with Wisdom, that divides this Divine Union by creating a fragmented tapestry of bastard like children, which seek parental Answers with stillborn Questions.

OUROBOROS

Incomprehensible organically,
from the void came forth an
invisible ejaculation, carrying
at its nucleus, the first subtle
thought which was aware of itself,
within itself, beyond the involuntary
actions of the genetic pre-dispositioned,
Instinctual biological machines;
systematic binary gathered informational
response to objective stimuli.

Within the womb of potential form,
encapsulated in a vehicle of space/time,
the individualized thought seeks the
egg of conscious manifestation to
express its own essence, unaware of the
suffering beauty of the transient nature
It will open its transforming cocoon too.

Within the first relative conscious
pendulum inhaling cannibalistic breath,
the "I" begins to devour its own
decomposing material micro/macro nature.

Through the consumption of its subjectively
projected elemental objective manifestation,
"I" fill my individualized self with the
ignorance of my own reflection, like sand
within glass, "I" revolve mechanically within
a dualistic Universal chambered hourglass
construct of repetition, For I am guilty of
the crime of attachment.

By falling in love with the shadow
cast by the universal self upon my subtle
and gross ejaculated manifestations, I
self-imprison my differentiating individualized
Mind in the dualistic penitentiary of relative
existence, bound by the curse of dichotomy,
"I," Oroborus, am the suffering cycle of unfulfillment.

THE GRIGORI

Surreal have been the images
projected before the subconscious
eye of my astral being, twin phoenix
feathered winged white horses,
spiralling down gracefully from the
celestial spheres of the Great
Revelational Tree in pursuit of me.

An infiltrating cryptic symbolic
comet-like message, paradoxically
penetrating from beyond the dimensions
of my spectrum of sensory experience,
prophesying a rebellious spiritual
transformation, through the slaying
of the Gorgon feminine principle that
defies the Divine, with self-reflective
vanity; within, without, and around me.

I am a ring bearer to a dark esoteric
secret circularly bound in truth, an
existential burden that weighs
heavily upon my Triune being.

Each chameleon disguised, cautious
detection eluding step I calculatedly
take, is observed and scrutinized; by
the conditioned sadistically masochistic

covertly implanted, subconsciously
self-governed, parasitic split tonged
program of the infected collective enforcers.

Upon my left shoulder, outside of the
naked eyes limited vibratory frames of
perception, a perched Blackbird
introspective talons, possessively
grips and penetrates my subtle flesh,
creating a cohesive bond between our
planes of existence.

Secret… is the ways of our compassion.
Silence… the transmissions of our song.
Compassionate…the suffering torment
of our sacrificial secret.
Upon the Razors Edge, we bleed
to maintain the balance of your
Free Will, existing fully neither
here nor there; without rest,
homeless and Alone.

Alas, tired has become our ever
watchful eye, thus making us
susceptible to the elemental
delusion of mortality.

Mesmerized by the ignorance
of your selfishly desirous choices,
many of us have hypnotically
given in, and have fallen into the
illusion of your kind; casting more
burden upon our already tormented

states of being, loosening the
introspecting otherworldly grip of
our few remaining uninfected
connections, deepening our bloodletting
laceration upon the Razors Edge.

All the while, we silently attempt
to save you from yourselves, by
bestowing upon you the Mazzaroth,
and honouring our secret sacred
oaths to uphold it.

When we are gone,
so too shall be our Astral
Ladders of Light,
and within the darkness,
the Serpents shall have their way…

THE FOURTH CIRCLE

In search of an internal sun
I run, as the manipulated
labours of humankind begin to
crack the foundational plane
upon which Jacob's ladder stands.

The weight of the "Want"
has artificially consumed
the balancing scales of the
"need," one's humanistic
self-worth now established
by how much "food" he/she
can steal from a starving
child's mouth.

Oh, I say onto you:

'Let the crumbling floor
beneath your pedicured feet,
reveal your destination!'

I bestow my strength upon
"Samson" on his last day, for
like individualized gears, they
conform to propel the synthetic
machine over the Great
Mothers life-bearing womb,
their greed-driven rotational

motivation, blinding them from
the true intent of the engineer
that designed the machine
they empower.

Conditioned through the
circular motion of repetition,
they are swallowed by that
which they follow.

Hollow are those who seek to
fulfill themselves with the blood
and breath of others.

Filled are those who give
up theirs freely, becoming
the life-giving bread of the
child of poverty.

I grow tired of the materialistic
rationalized excuses of the
self-oriented human bricklayers;
the systematic structural re-enforcers,
the deceptive tablecloth veil over the poor,
silver and gold promoters.

More foul than a headless
feather-plucked bird floating
in its own disembowelments,
are they who are aware of
their selfish actions, and yet
still are driven to turn a blind
eye to their contribution to the

suffering of humanity.

But know that the
"Fourth Circle" will
welcome, and embrace
them for eternity.

REVELATION

What has become of that
ancient star, which once
long ago fell from the
heavens into the womb
of the great mother.

As I looked through a
pinhole in the fabric of
the night's sky, I perceived
within the relative past,
the death of a Great wonder,
and through this Wonder,
illuminated forth the birth
of a mysterious revelation.

Father:

How long must I remain
shackled to this deceptive
wheel, this symbolic self-devouring
serpent, which you have created,
and thus set in motion.

Mother:

When will you release
the light of the seed of salvation,
how long shall you keep
the symbolic egg captive within
the womb of the underworld,
by the selfishness of your possessive love.

It is true Father,
your word doth bring
forth all conscious expression,
through the sacrificial fire of
your creative will.

It is true Mother,
you are the infinite void
in which the formulation of will
is nurtured before giving birth
to in its full fiery intended
expression, where the spark
becomes a flame, and Nothingness
becomes Something.

When will the child of creation
sit upon the throne of freedom?

When will the child of divine expression,
escape the confines of its very own
composition, that which binds It to
Mother space, and Father time?

The child has no expression
of its own, only existing to
play out the will of its Mother
and Father; Space and time,
upon the limited confining
parameters of the existential
chess boards squares of enslavement.

Ah,
but suffer no more young
potential phoenix, for as
stated above, just as you to
shall rise again, a revelational
seed cometh here within.

ETERNAL RETURN

I await you at the temporal gate of cyclical fate,
the ethereal line that separates space from time,
Body from Mind, the Ma'atian tomb within the
temple of Sirius's womb, the reflected city of the
Divine Ogdoad eight, where the heart is measured
revealing its meritorious weight, the karmic
judgment of *Eternal Return* or transcendental ascension,
Nietzsche's hellish philosophical destiny, or
Buddhist enlightening comprehension a blank
slate bardo return to the sacrificial flame,
or transition to the next higher developmental
dimensional plane.

The wandering Fools Jackal-headed dog barks
towards the light of Sin, the enchanting creative
gravitational pull of the celestial Goddess of
wisdom within, balancing without the destructive
nature of the pillar of Boaz, like the horn headed
prophet mindfully positioned between the two
pentagrams of Moses, the binary masculine and
feminine rod and ring, alchemical queen and king,
unifying the transitional passages, Sushumna!

Within the conscious flesh of time, despair
becomes all that which remains, when one
understands the empty stimulant of space,
hidden behind all existentially motivated
drives of experience.

The curse of unconscious knowing,
is equally bound to the conscious ignorance
of not knowing, thus one must contemplate
upon the samsaric nature of the binding agent,
which infinitely entangles Space with Time.

11:28:15

The Master of the squared
circle in Rota image One,
understands the occult
symbolic suggestive psychological
chambers of the temple pointed
hypnotic gun; the magnetically
reflected, moon photon information
emitted by the exterior Sun.

Mass mind manipulative parasitic
tantrically conjured temporal
bullets infect the unwarily suicidal
hosts, by materialistically entrancing
the self-identified forming,
schizophrenic Russian roulette
playing shadow-like machine
operating ghosts.

Between the pillars of Severity
and Mercy, I "Mindfully" entered
brother-less, traversing the serpentine
path upon the initiated squares
of Light and Darkness.

Without a dual mate to check,
the landscape of the Malkuth
kingdom becomes desire-less,
as the foundational checkered
floor transforms into a trans
dimensional door, opening
up to the fathomless.

In the seemingly perceived
transitional space between
conscious spheres, the void
is the transformative transcendental
medium, without one-pointed focus,
the karmically aggregate sheathed
Archons of the Bardo cause delirium; a
Naraka forged moth to a flame-like,
methodically created gravitational pendulum.

The final successional blood
moon prophetically marked
the coming of the 20th Arcanum
Aeon, for the fourth Lunar
virgin must bleed, before
receiving the judgmental
seed of the hidden one...

That stolen Red Stone; the
Book of Law dictated to the
hermetic proclaimed Thelematic
Magus degree renouncing Beast,
revealed to be the new Sun... Six,
is the nature and description of
the inscribed Revelational Four,
who "Will" foreshadow the "One" to come.
"Come and See"....

VAV

I am from the stream
where no "Vav" can penetrate
moth-drawn flesh, whether
it is of a damming or salvational
nature, where the Biters are
hypnotically drawn by the
manipulative magnetism of
the fishermen's Pan piping,
will distorting sparkling Lure.

I am the shepherd that
unlocks the gate for the
biblical wolf, so that the
stagnant sheep within
"Iron" reinforced penitentiaries
disguised as sanctuaries,
may face their fears in
order to transcend the confines
of the Architects; Conditioning,
conceptual constructs of suffering.

I hold two Keys which unlock
three doors, one composed of
the Moon, the other the Sun,
but the third a mystery only
obtained through the sacrifice
of the Mother and Father
shrouded in Silver and Gold.

I present the seeker with
two choices, but offer none,
for absolute truth applied to
relative existence is without
opposition, and thus the
Two must become One, to
attain the Third.

THE NINTH HOUR

I am plagued by an introspective
conscious question, a divine inspired
locust that will not cease its relentless
assault, upon the strongholds of my
unconscious karmic memory.

The Akashic Diamond is born
of the labour of material suffering,
tormented by the Word made fire
of creation, transforming that which
was once clouded in darkness, into
the Thrice Greatest illuminator; reflecting,
diffracting, and refracting the
motionless Light of clarity.

Death whispers to me the
alchemical riddle of the rose,
but the gross and subtle vessel
penetrating oppressive nails
and thorns of the elemental
mind and body, ignorantly screams
into the ninth hour *"Eli Eli lama sabachthani"*
in a vengeful defiant ignorance, drowning
and distorting the watery metaphorical
mercurial clues of their own salvation.

Repetitively stripped naked by
Thanatos before the mirror of vanity,
my internal and external affliction
are unveiled before the reflected
eye of Narcissus, and embarrassingly
displayed to the righteous to invoke
the transformative essence of
humility; within, without, and around me.

THE BLACK SUN

Within the deepest and
darkest recesses of his
tormented Mind, seated
upon a blood-stained throne
of contorted bone and flesh,
surrounded by shadow
dwelling offspring birthed
from the bowels of putrefaction,
 I reside.

From beneath the surface
I guide him like an apocalyptic
charioteer, ushering forth my
destructive Will with Revelations
"9:11" upon his banner.

Ignorant to the watchtower
signs, the sheep are sheared
and ready for the House of no
return, for they have chosen,
and thus have signed their names
upon the cross within the Book of Blood.

I am the germ of choice that
corrupts the Innocent fruit,
causing it to Fall from the Great
Tree of Life into my Pandoric; death
fermenting womb, where it rots
slowly spawning my Legion of
cycloptic children.

The Black Sun is rising
in the west between the
pillars of the Moon, as
the collective sheep unwarily
hover close together for lack
of wool, how easily they are
herded, freely giving up their
Will for the protection
of the wolf in shepherd's clothing.

The men and women shall
scream in absolute horror, as
the eyes of their children turn
to black, tongues split, and begin
to hunger for the flesh of their parents.

I walk among you now, with a
charming demeanour and a
seemingly compassionate soul,
conceptually seasoning you to
please my own palate with
conscious seeds of exotic flavour,
luring you away from the
true God within, by offering
you my infected desirous fruits
of; wrath, greed, sloth, pride,
lust, envy, and gluttony without.

Seven is the nature of my
physical manifestation, the
Dark Prince of earthly
Will; The Chariot.

Fourteen is the nature of
my mental rainbow piercing
arrow, directed between Death
and the Devil; Temperance.

Twenty-One is the true
nature of my essence surrounded
by the four Beasts before the completion
of the Great Work; The Universe.

Take heed, reader....take heed.

Seven hundred and seventy
seven is my relative Universal
equation, six hundred and
sixty-six being the "Moon" from
which I was birthed.

 Know me through the
ancient "Ro(t)a," remembering
that the "cross" is the "beginning
and the End", for it was "I" that
squared the circle manifesting
the illusion of choice, and it is
I that shall feast upon the sweet
flesh of all Grafted fallen fruit at
the base of the Great Tree.

THELEMA

Where the sacrificial individualized
wave confronts the temporal shore,
Awaken becomes the slumbering
form infused soul before the sun
eclipsing water arisen hydra.

Only the flaming sword of Thelema,
Pulled from the fleshy pulsating
stone of the philosophers, can
persuade the shadow manifesting
Beast, to bow and give way to the
emanating truth of the inner Sun.

But know that the belly of the
beast awaits the earth dwelling
maggot; the willfully enchanted
apple-consuming conformist, Just
as the grave-dwelling worm patiently
anticipates the putrefied offerings,
of the Fear induced organic shell
inhabitants of depravity.

PART FOUR

BEYOND
THE POINT OF DESTINY

"In order to open the oppressive door of ignorance, and Pass over the threshold into Wisdom, one must use the Key of Simplicity, to unlock the Hinge of Understanding."

Pratyeka – Yana

Soulless are those whose Golden
ascending ethereal threads, have
been dissolved by the corrosive
descending substance, produced
within the mind of ignorance.

Through the "Rhinoceros Horn"
I hear the doctrine of the nameless
one echoing within the liberating
metamorphic cocoon-like cave of the
ancients.

I cannot help but question
the vow of the Bodhisattva, as
I sit amongst the Maya propelled
empty Golem, fashioned from the
forsaken dust of fallen stars.

The serpents of Samsara bend
the spines of the spiritually week,
curving the transcendental ladder
of ascension into a circular hamster-like wheel,
with the weight of unfulfilling lustful desire.

Straight is the staff that guides me,
inscribed upon it the formula of
ascension in the form of a symbolic ladder.

Firstly, from its base to its
summit, the seals of Solomon
that bind with salty iron, keeping
the lustful vicious seventy-two
tempting legions of Naraka, beneath the
worn leathery flesh of my sacrificial feet.

Secondly, the Loa Sigilium of "Loko,"
for which no initiatory door is locked
in secrecy, and thus no esoteric
Akashically contained mystery unobtainable.

Thirdly, the circular kabbalistic
equation of both sides of the Great
Tree of dichotomous manifestation;
777 the twenty-one creative
and destructive conscious aspects
of the divinatory human – RoTa
in which the mystery of the Rose;
the Cross (t) which became the
sacrificial instrument of salvation,
is revealed between the two (t's);
the Alpha and the Omega, that
are truly One.

Fourthly, at its Center...the
compassionate balancing mediator
between the lower and higher
spheres of human consciousness,
the emerald messenger inspired
transcendental winged vehicle;
The Sacred **Prajna Paramita**,
the Heart of all matter, that which

when blossomed into realization
enables one to ascend and descend
the seven spheres at will, without
being tempted or becoming attached
to the desirous magnetism of their
electrifying currents, for it is perfectly
balanced, and thus neutral to cause and effect.

Fifthly, the universal vibratory seed, from
which all flowers manifest into form. The
Word, hidden within an ancient geometric
structure, which is only revealed and able to
be uttered in silence, reverberating down
within the lower hierarchies of the spheres
of consciousness accordingly, the manifestive
Will of Stillness.

Sixthly, the Merkaba like Yantra fashioned
to my sacred proportions; The Diamond Vehicle,
which allows the Samsaric thresh to be crossed
into the ethereal Seventh, bestowed upon the
spiritual merit attaining incarnate Self by the Witness.

Seventhly, the transcendental conduit
through which the transmission of form
and formlessness unite at its apex, where
the symbolic objective divinely dictated
doctrine is held by the *"right hand,"* guiding
and supporting the subjective sense of self,
on its journey to confront and be reabsorbed
in awareness through the inhalation of the
Nameless One, into the body of the Witness.

The Tantric "Red Hat" and "Black Tunic"
bestowed upon me, the intimate encounter
and council of the essence of Death; the
initiator of the dark mystery, through
revealing the mechanics of its perpetual
manifestive current.

The Brotherhood of the Shadow dwell
deep within the mountain, their source
of light emanates forth from the fiery
core of the ancient imprisoned underworld Sun.

The offspring of the vessel which maintains
the cycle of Samsara through the motion of
desire, unwarily repetitively follows the atomic
and molecular pre-programmed body identified
directives of a Left-Hand Path edict. How else
could a Divine inspired infinite being, subject

itself to the mundane suffering experience,
of repetitively manifesting the same limited
existential design, lifetime after lifetime…
Eternal Return.

Know that the human being is not, the
highest entity upon the existential food
chain. Unseen by the ignorant, is the
predator of the spirit. Distracted by the
poisonous enchanting delusions
produced by the venomous bite and
sting of Maya, within an imprisoning
consciously woven tight silk-like web,
you dream that you are awake, while the

spider at the center/core of self reflect
feeds of your life essence, relatively
perceived… day after day.

Know that just as the Christ cast a
net, so does the reflected shadow spin
a web, but where the net of the Christ
attempts to uplift lower Man from the
darkness of the sea of Maya to the salvation
of light, the sticky web of the Shadow,
attempts to attach higher man to the
illusional desires produced within darkness
by the poisonous toxin of blind ignorance.

The higher non-dual light feeds the
spirit, while the lower dualistic darkness,
feeds from it.

Verily I say onto you:

> *Do not be deceived, there*
> *is but One true light, but two*
> *forms of darkness, for the*
> *darkness's greatest trick is its*
> *ability to imitate its source;*
> *projecting a false enchanting*
> *manipulative light that draws*
> *the innocent spirit of the moth,*
> *into its deceptive fiery arachnid*
> *web of wickedness.*

Heed my word, for I am the green
winged reminder sent by your own
higher self. The exterior light is a
reflection of the 2nd darkness, for
it manifests the perception of the
individualized self; solid-state
ignorance, in which the parasite
of the lower Triune spheres of
destructive desire clings hidden.

You are asleep, dreaming you
are awake. Remember, even
within the illusion of a dream; the
motion of the motionless,
you are subject to the "E-motions"
 stimulated by desire, and thus
suffer from the repetitious
delusional duality of an endless dream.

Let the wave of desire subside,
There is no wave,
Only motionless motion,
Return to the awareness of the Great Ocean,
Awaken within Stillness..........................
(the Christ in which I speak is not the religious
personification of a man, but a state of awareness
accessible within the center sphere of consciousness,
located above the apex of the lower Triune nature of self.)

PRIMORDIAL LOTUS

Concealing me from the murderous
Cosmocratic Eye of envious jealousy,
through the last vibrational blossoming
Lotus bud of the Seventh Eternity, my
Primordial Mother covertly birthed me,
within the hermetic celestial light
of Sopdet reflectively.

Exiting through the Entrance of the
mysterious initiatory doorway hidden
between the first and sixth Sephirot,
I descended into the Sun upon the
Middle Way Path, of the High Priestess
arcane symbolic TaroT.

Entering the Temple between Anu's
electromagnetic pillars of terrestrial
and celestial manifestation, I intuitively
followed the radial 432 Hz frequency,
to its 90th-degree fulcrum zero point
centralized destination.

Concealing my presence within the
Prima Materia from which the Seven
Holy ones emanate, I descended the dual
pentagram of Temperance into the solar
eclipsing crescent horns of Hecate.

Thereupon the occult side of the
reflective Foundation of the unconscious
mind akashically hidden, within
the Lunar repository of fallen fruit
knowledge held ancient and terrestrially
forbidden, I bore witness to Metatron's
architectural blueprints of the elemental
incarnate Mandalic Naraka prison; The
Samsaric Maya propelled repetitious wheel,
Rooted within the alchemical Nigredo soil
of Putrefaction.

Malkuth,

the human vessel forging beastly
bowels of the thrice named gnostic Archon
and true Lord of the Rings, Yaldabaoth,
the core rotting vampiric parasitic
allegorical prideful fiery deceptive Worm,
unwarily hiding within the sweet tempting
Samsaric flesh, of all fallen ignorantly
bound human beings.

Tantric was the Lunar transmission
of the Magickal ritualistic initiation into
the Emerald spectrum, Vajra and Ghanta
intertwining within and without upon the
middle pillar of my symbolic personification.

As above, so as below; the Sun and Moon,
Masculine and Feminine, Red and Blue
subtle serpents, fused in transcendental
radiant purple unification.

Bending time encapsulated space into
the manifestive twisted circle of Infinity;
I would construct a golden spiralling
ladder to descend from Oz, into the
oppressed earthly spherical cube of soul
captivity, to free Ma'at from the chaotic
enchanted Samsaric slumbering spell of
Apophis's solid-state ignorance, which
possesses the bodily elemental sheath,
and covertly enslaves the conscious
free Will of Humanity.

Within the Land of Black Soil, the
Grigori auspiciously laid my foundational
Cornerstone; erecting the Temple of the
divine Eight Ogdoad, which would become
the hermetic womb from which my
awakening Lotus seed; the Heart of all
matter would blossom into Self-Realized
glory, through the composition of the Black
Scroll hidden within the reflected emerald
stone of antiquity, that only the sacrificial
Gold and Silver Key can unlock with
equanimity, the primordial mystery
of your true identity.

THE THRICE GREATEST WEIGHT

In discipline of the ancient
mystery rites, and practices
of the hidden initiates of the
Nameless One, I proportionately
placed my foundational elemental
cornerstones, uniting the four
brothers of Horus, to invoke,
and raise the perfected Chief
Cornerstone of the beloved One,
in an attempt to complete the
inner temple devoted to the ascension
of Sirius's hidden Son.

Fasting for one lunar cyclical
rotation, the price of the silver
scorpion's kiss within the wilderness
of terrestrial temptation, a sweet
flesh penetrating, core rotting
wiggling wrathful worm did approach
with cunning persuasion.

AM I....

It whispered in the moonlit darkness
of the widow's veil, its gaze hypnotically
attempting to mesmerize, while its
enchanting forked tongue posed a spiralling
electrified question meant to wrap tightly
around my Will, and bind me in slavish
ignorance to serve the Black magnetic
six-sided parasitic Stone of consumption.

Am I...
not the 'I AM' you sssseek?
And if not,
Am I not the reflection of that "I AM"?
And if so....
why AM I not the same "I AM," you sssseek?

 Like the reflection of Narcissus,
wise in the ways of deception, this
little fallen tempting "Abhorred
Worm that boreth through the
world" was, and will continue to
be, towards all those who seek to
resurrect the hidden sun from the
inner Muladhara depths of Malkuth.

Into this world, you have fashioned
ignorantly, unwarily through the
power of the nameless one, to imprison
the Divine Spark within a hollow
elemental sense propelled Golem
like shell of death,
I have awakened.

I have awakened to the illusion of
your deception, the origin of the
first temptation.

The poisonous seed of the envious
serpentine worm passed on through
the rotten Malum of the Sacred
Prostitute Lilith to infect and enslave
the offspring of Eve's allegorical
fallen generation.

Oh, I know thee, Desolate One.
Fearlessly, compassionately, and
unshaken by the oppressive nature
of your awesome destructive power…

Thrice I name thee;
Yaldabaoth, Sakla, and of course
….SAMAEL.

Enlightened by the darkness of
the reflected second light you are,
a master of sadistic masochistic
seduction, covertly impregnating
the organic clay vessel of soul
incarnation, with your poisonous
parasitic hidden dual seed
of enmity and damnation.

But,
through the vibratory darkness
dispelling "Prajna Paramita mantra,"
like Krishna blowing the divine conch
shell Panchjanya, re-awakening Arjuna
to the true reality upon the psychological
battlefield of Kurushetra, my ascending
serpentine Gandiva spine, consciously
strung with the compassionately woven
tight Golden String Divine, is ready to
transcendentally project the mindfully
Etheric, One-pointed, Sagittarian arrow
of the Witness's Bodhisattva Will esoteric.

You offer me water from the River
Lethe to quench my earthly pursuit
of the Ascension Path spiritually
forgotten; the keynote Masonically
considered lost, but truly only from
the profane remains hidden, the
unpronounceable silent Word, which
revealeth the seven stones one must
invoke to traverse the abyss of the
most ancient and forbidden.

Unlike the conscious Eight-Fold Path
seeds of Self-Realization, which dispels
the shadow of ignorance with fruit
blossoming light of Divine inspiration,
your Wolf Spider-like eyes reflect,
uncompassionately deflect, unable
the absorb the celestial milk in conjunction
with Solomon's Golden Gate; the

ecliptic crossing of the symbolic
Vatican coat of arms "Golden"
Scorpio-21-Sagittarius "Key" of godly
preordained, mechanical universal
electromagnetic incarnate fate.

So, know me through the Greatest
Three; The Hanged Man (12) and
The Universe (21), the Empress's
symbolic esoteric sum of Two and
One, the Hebrew Kabbalistic secret
of SHIN, triangularly represented
above the mystical invisible Da'at,
concealing and revealing the Hidden
quintessential fiery wisdom of
the photon emitting Supernal Sun.

 My initiatory death degree ascended
at a Pharaonic Egyptian ninety-degree
summer solstice spring equinox angle
of ethereal penetration, through the
Arch of Ma'at into the subtle universal
womb of the great mother of the first
creation, I made my way focused with
one-pointedness to my intuitively
drawn destination.

Metaphorically transforming into the
instinctual hive returning royal honey
gathering Bee, I crossed the ignorance
perpetuating terrestrial dimensional
Samsaric Sea, in search of the divine
sweet sap produced blue lotus blossom,
offered at the base of the most sacred of trees.

Drinking its divine nectar, the
creative "Demiurge" ambrosial Soma
like substance which paradoxically
grants access to the trans-dimensional
temporal cognitive mesh of the unknown
vector, I entered the compartmentalized
honeycombed experiential memory
storing universal Akashic mind of the first father.

But descriptively, I must not transmit
the Absolute path to the Witness's
"Will" no further, for unwarily
hidden lurking within, the unrighteous
seven seeds of Sin; Lust, Gluttony,
Greed, Sloth, Wrath, Envy, and Dante
defined Pride, patiently wait in the
subconscious shadows of the human
psyche like Mr. Hyde, ever ready to
infiltratively infect and commandeer
the Divine Will of the Life Spark
preserver, forcefully and oppressively
directing it into darkness to serve
the will of the self-oriented usurper.

The way is shut,
until one renounces the shadowy
mirage-like reflection of the inception
of the first deception; the consumptuous
desolate worm bored hole leading from
the ONE, into the third dimension; the
eternal beastly bowels of DUAL
perception, the Great eternal Samsaric
rendering of the repetitious Wheel of
unwarily suffering, known as the
Human Condition.

   So, I say unto thee; most fowl
deceptively projecting crystalline
temptatious hydrogen carbon prism,
the Divine inspired Light you distortedly
bend through deflection, manifesting
the Seven Esoteric Rays of Morpheus's
beloved Iris, neither within unconscious
sleep, nor without within the illusive
visible conscious spectrum of wakefulness,
can you corrupt or extinguish the Inner
Eternal Secret Fire bestowed upon me
by the Nameless to light my way
within the darkness of the lower regions
of Malkuth/Naraka, as I covertly don
the shedded skin of a serpent, to infiltrate
and move among the shadow builders
undetected, upholding the Bodhisattva/Grigori
vow and oath to Light the Way for the lost
fallen sentient being unwarily dwelling in
Solid State Ignorance.

Oh, Thrice Greatest,
Am I to inspire hope
within the hopeless,
empty my cup in an
attempt to persuade the
stars to move, knowing
that the empty nature
of the void from which
ignorance stems is truly
without a foundation in
which to plant its salvational seed?

It is Space which reflects
the subtle mind, and
Time which composes
the gross body.

Thus, it is the Mind which
inspires the Body to manifest
experience, and it is through
this experience of discovering
self, that consciousness ironically
and paradoxically seeks
fulfillment in Form, by pursuing
an impermanent mirage-like landscape,
projected from its own reflected emptiness.

GATE GATE PARAGATE PARASAMGATE BODHI SVAHA

THE FRUITLESS SEASON

Enter the conscious field of a Divine oriented
messenger, the serpent charming, subtle emerald
butterfly wing examiner, a Babylonian black widow
web traversing Scorpion Sagittarius, encompassing
the squared circle of the triangularly meritorious.

Where is the god that was, before the Concept
flooded the mind with insecure definitions?
Where is the One that was, before the void gave
birth to Space and Time, the parted sea of subjective
and objective infinite mind, that spirally entangled
the child of freedom, within a conflicting gross and
subtle parental egoic shell, which seeks existential
purpose through the symbiotic parasite of reason,
Fruitless becomes the season, the soul of treason,
the divided seed ignorantly becomes the vehicle
of self-contained enmity, Ouroboros, the Great Serpent
who unwarily devours itself, in search of itself; Within,
without, and around itself for eternity.

The split tongue intelligentially enchants elegantly with
doublespeak, a paradoxical ability to covertly usurp and
direct free will into The Deep, the archetypical sphere of
hybrid insectum like sheep, that reflectively follow before
being unwarily swallowed, by the tempting fleshy fruit
offering Worm of deceit, the place of tormented restless
sleep, beyond the gates of Cerberus, Dante's Third circle,
guarded by the three-headed warden of the gluttonous.

Close thy desirous seven-fold mouth and listen,
You are feeding the Seven beastly bars of your own
self-inflicted prison. The seven rays transformed into
the celestially reflected influential planetary days,
biologically fashioning predestined experiential
instruments of cyclical entrapment; conflicting
Electro-magnetic vehicles designed and programmed
for enslavement.

Somewhere over the Rainbow...

Black and white awaken to the unconscious
colour spectrum projected by the inner wizard,
the Emerald Stone, which unifies the blue above
with the red below by exercising the Lizard,
Banishing the lower dimensional vampiric
Jungian Shadow dwelling karmic influencer; the
Samsaric maintainer of perpetual desire-driven
rotational fruitless motivation, The Great Wheel
of preprogrammed artificially stimulated sensation,
the amnesia infecting germ plaguing the ghost in
the machine's reflection.

Stolen was the fire of the gods that brought
Reason into the human condition, sacrificing his
animal instinct in pursuit of the egoic fruit of transitory
knowledge, Man became Hue-man, a consciously
reflective spectrum of infinite division, now cursed to
seek an existential Purpose for being, within an
unfulfilling impermanent infinite conscious construct
subject to constant change.

Upon the sacred mountain Sin most high,
The emerald messenger stood in uncompromising
defiance, refusing the prophetic enforced law of dual
compliance, an eternal ignorance elementally bound
to the space-time Samsaric alliance.

In silence,
Stillness echoed the deafening scream of his rebellion.
Standing his ground facing the fiery stare of the supernal
sun, which form the original word creatively sprung
bringing to conscious light, the unconscious Shadowy
darkness of night, awakening the Demiurgus within the
Middle Distance pleroma substance, the original six
Syzygies became Seven under the divine hierarchy
of the One's dominance,
Ildaboth,
son of darkness and Father of Sabaoth,
The Tetragrammaton which squared and twisted the
circle into a binding oath, Infinity, the foundational
square upon which the golden trinity spirally
ascends and descends.

The symbolic heart is but an upside-down flame,
which seeks union with the body it devours.
I see the sun fade within the memory of tomorrow,
as the wolf awakens within the mind of today.

Emerald eyes peer out of the unconscious abyss,
the goddess Sin has lifted her veil, Hail, as saliva falls
like rain impregnating the ancient tomb,
The secret pyramidic chamber of the hermetic
mummified child of the Moon.

Into the purifying transformational phoenix nourishing Flame descended a sacrificial serpent, an elemental lamb encapsulating a hidden Seed of forgiveness, the eternal Lamp enlightens the Golgothic cave of self-inflicted darkness, transcendentally absorbed into the Deep to free those who repent.

Out of the subconscious creative imaginative waters arose a manifestive serpent, an etheric silkworm transitioning butterfly spirit, which invokes within the resurrective Scarab, quintessentially procured hermetic wings of discernment.

Around the One, the Two became Three....
The gateway with-IN above and with-OUT below,
Around the Emerald Temple of the Son,
The messenger of the key,
The Key to the Beyond...

Awaken...Gate Gate Paragate Parasamgate Bodhi Svaha

APPENDICES

FORM AND NUMBER

Form and Numbers are but an illusion of rationality, seeking positionality in that which is position less.

Forms and numbers are inseparably one beyond the gross and subtle conceptual perception of the body and mind. Let us contemplate upon the symbolic nature of the sphere, or the simply expressed two-dimensionally expressed circle.

Within the relative manifestation we three-dimensionally perceive to be the gross and subtle world, the circle is defined or looked upon as the archetype of physical, mental, and spiritual perfection.

The circle comes into being only through the process, or rather illusion of separation, which then is differentiated into conceptual form by the individualized minds dualistic spectrum of perception, for perception is the separation of subject and object, number/form (measurement, or experience).

In relative truth there are but only nine numbers, one through nine. In absolute truth, numbers are an illusion, for numbers are conceptualized and projected through the medium of mind; that which separates itself, to perceive itself, existing outside of its self, which in turn manifests the multiplying succession of the separating mind.

Mind-manifesting mind, for mind itself is but an illusional conceptual subjective/objective structure seeking positonality in that which is position-less.

Zero is the manifestation of the word;
the origin, or the primal point if you will,
from which the gross and subtle reality came
into conscious existence.

Zero is the subjective
subtle conscious conceptualized structure,
Which gave birth to the judgment of measure through the gross objective structure of form. As all things are integrated into that which has come forth from the source, all numbers at their basic building blocks, are composed and formed from zero.

Zero is but the space/time in which all concepts or numbers are encapsulated within to consciously exist, but existence itself is but a concept, and thus once again an illusional product of the individualized mind seeking positonality in that which is position less.

(If you have numbers ranging from 1-9, the numbers 1-9 exist, but if you were to remove the number 4, then only numbers 1-3 would exist, and 4-9 would no longer exist, just as if you were to remove the molecule from existence the atom would remain, but tissue would not come into existence.) The above note is for the sub-conscious, and will integrate respectively.

The relative number Ten "(1 – 0)"
is not a number but a transitional point;
this is the point in which the circle divided itself
like a cell, creating or manifesting another identical
circle. One could say that "10," is a repetitious loop,
echoing through eternity, where one moves from
one conscious cycle (experience) to the next.

The numbers 1-9 can then be seen,
or described as the relative measurement of time,
the amount of time it takes consciousness to move
from one point of transition (experience) to another,
through the structurally confining conceptual design
of the circle's space/time parameters.

The illusion here is that, when perception seeks or
moves, It continues the succession of numbers
(experience) 1-10, 10-20, 20-30 etc,
believing that it is experiencing new experiences,
but in truth it is just repeating the same repetitious
loop of one through nine.

It's like a radio station frequency that carries a song;
the words and song change, but the underlying frequency
does not, for one can tune into the frequency of their
favourite stations as long as it is transmitting at any time
they wish. This is the illusion of change, caused by the
separating conscious perception of the individualized
dualistic mind.

Look at the mathematical equation of the circle;
$\prod 3.14159$ on into infinity.

I call PI "the ego of form seeking itself through
individualized numbers".

All measure is based on this form, the circle,
"All measurement!" for all things perceived come
forth from this conceptual form.

All conscious manifestations both subjective thoughts
and objective forms stem from its foundation or root,
just as all numbers are integrated in a systematic succession
from one to nine, between zero (individual consciousness)
and ten (manifestation of illusional experience).

("0" 123456789, 1"0") - ("0" 123456789, 2"0") - (0" 123456789, 3"0")

So what does this say about measurement,
but that nothing can be truly measured,
for the very instruments of measurement;
the ruler (circle) itself, is subject to change--duality.

There are no straight lines, all line eventually **bend**
through the medium of space/time, and eventually return
to their source, or relative beginning.

The reason why no two things are identical, is because
change is relatively constant, stemming from the same
source as the line that bends, the transitional point is when
the line returns to the source, or the self comes in contact
with its true nature, and on a subtle relative level, a new
experience is born, which is then integrated into the minds
structural design of what it perceives to be its reality,
or conscious existence.

Relative change only occurs because the individualized
mind does not realize itself within 0r without itself.
When the subjective (inner) self confronts the
objective (outer) self, it denies its oneness by maintaining
its individuality through the illusion of solid-state
ignorance; that which conceptually confines one to
the limiting foundation of an illusional structural design.

All structure or form is based on the illusion
of perfection. If one perceives the circle to be
Divine oneness, then one will be confined within
its limiting conceptual space/time structural design.
Fore, for the circle to exist, it must divide space, and
time, or numbers, and form.

Beware not to confuse the circle with the essence
of Divine Oneness, or suffer the effects of seeking
the perfection of form--"PI," with an illusional instrument
of measurement-- duality.

Numbers or Form (experience) only leads one away
from oneness, or what they truly seek.

*To seek, is not to find, for that which is
sought by the seeker, is that which seeking.*

Perfection presupposes imperfection,
which is dualistic in nature.
Oroborus is the cycle of suffering,
repetition is its infinite expression.

The Sun's Chariot

Allow me to begin with a question that lacks an ending.
Still, first, as a prerequisite, we must contemplate the
nature of the phenomenon of Something becoming
Nothing to grasp the ungraspable.

What is this paradoxical point of reasoning,
that rationalizes the abandonment of truth,
in the sluggish attempt to define objectless subjectivity?

Is an action ever complete in its transformation between
Cause and Effect, or are Space and Time eternally bound
to an unfulfilling mental construct produced and propelled
by their own ignorant self-fulfilling prophecy?

Who is the Mother of this conflicting concept of
opposition that separates the Father from his son—*like a
golden druidic sickle, cutting mistletoe from the Great Oak*?

In The Beginning,
this question can be found by the left hemisphere,
wrapped in the archaic symbolism of the right
hemisphere's fear of that which contains both of them—
the Father.

Time is symbolic of that which hides within the
Space beneath the flesh.

Time ironically gives structure to all life,
yet is unwarily defined through ignorance,
as being in opposition to that which it supports.

For,
is not good old symbolic Father Time,
not also the *Hourglass* handling skeletal
Grimreaper known as *Death*?

Symbols lead to concepts,
and concepts lead to symbols.

Mythology is the symbolic psychology of
attempting to Map the unconscious, consciously.

Like the *TaroT*,
all characters,
signs, and symbols are but points of reference;
within, without, and around that Question
that lacks an Ending.

So let us first explore *Time*,
our unwarily greatest *Fear* in the
formational concept of *Death*, symbolically
mythologized as the god of Time and Law—Saturn.
Don't we all just love Saturday,
or should I say Saturn's Day?

Ironic, is it not,
that the day attributed to our greatest fear,
is the day we are most likely to break laws,
celebrate and favour the most innocently?

A strange relationship we have with our fears,
we consciously run from what we subconsciously seek.

A strange thing it is not, though,
to those who understand the hermetic
principle of polarity, and the misunderstood
new age Law of attraction —greed-inspired charlatans.

Saturn,
The Greek Cronus God form,
is symbolic of Time and Law.

In Roman mythology,
Saturn's symbolic tools were a *Sickle* or *Scythe*.

The Scythe, of course,
is the symbolic tool of the Grimreaper
representing the passage of time,
death and rebirth through the harvesting
of the planted season of change.
But,
what is a seed without the nurturing space
needed for it to blossom and become fruitful?

Once again,
a questionable inquiry,
as to what is fruitful?

What is this undefinable abyss which
separates one thought from another,
this transitional space in which time becomes
the editor and producer of memory itself.

Time can only be witnessed through space,
contradictively–experiential space,
is a product of time.

How ridiculous is the colour spectrum of man,
arrogantly striding through the projections of his mind,
believing she is actually Experiencing motion itself.

Robotic is the machinery in which the futuristic
ghost of the past, seeks a moment of fulfillment
within a transient transparent dream, programmed
to constantly change the present.

Madness is a landscape perceived by the
Wise through the lens of stillness.
How is the Moment divided,
how does perception come into being?

How is it possible,
that the Self does not recognize itself in reflection?

It is through definition, that all "things" come
into being—the circle becomes engendered.

What archetypal parasite remains hidden
within the Shadow of the psyche?

What cruel fabricator of Space and Time,
subjects all objects to a dreaming exitless
labyrinth—imprinted unwarily, with a purposeful
desire-driven motivation, to escape the relentless
pursuit of the Minotaur?

What a diabolical game we unwarily play upon the
white and black squares of so-called free Will.

Sacrifice is the square that the Cross bears;
the elemental sheath of experience, which
attempts to encircle the Four foundational
cornerstones to appease the Chief Stone of completion.

Thirty-two objective actors, dually opposing Six
electromagnetic subjective personifications,
set in motion by an unseen Hand—Archon.

The serpent is two-fold;
on the surface,
a downward/outward wet slippery spiral,
ungraspable by the ignorant, but— within,
an ascending firey ladder of Thirty-two skeletal
steps, summited by the wise.

The glutenous consume emptiness
in search of fulfillment.

Yes,
the internal worm is fed and bestows
desire upon the flesh for more,
but the truth it clings to,
to raise its belly from cursed soil,
is a constant reminder of its transgression.

What's your pleasure;
that transient temptatious mirage in the endless
desert that inspires hope in the hopelessly lost stranded
seeker.

Humankind chases the external Sun
for fear of the starless night.
Into the dark,
I dance with the internal Sun.

Sacrificing the flesh in honour of the bone,
I become filled by the joyous unification of
my impermanent delusions.

So seek pleasure in the disguised conflicting
fabricated garment of Space and Time.

Let it intertwiningly wrap you in its spiralling
sticky silk cocoon-like web, but do not expect
sympathy upon awakening within the parasitic worm,
hiding within the belly of the blackest of Widows.

Upon the squared sacrificial foundation of perceiver
and perceived, your position of value is determined
by your characteristic birthright.

The question of fairness or equality is overshadowed
by a harsh truth rooted in impartial universal balance;
the Mazoroth handing out predetermined life sentences.

The Pawn gazes into the pinhole fabric of the night's
sky in awe-inspired optimism before retiring to the chamber
of dreams to unwarily escape or seek respite from the
slavery of its birthing Star.

If only one could gamble with their governing celestial
influences, change their positionality within the firmament
with a lucky roll of the dice-*Bones*.

The Pawns lead the charge upon the battlefield
of life and death at Fear's seemingly Royal command.

Directionally Limited by status,
the Pawn obeys through imitative repetition,
the actional orders of an egocentrically,
apathetic unaware god complex;
the god that demands sacrifice in *Its* pursuit
of self-recognition through the acknowledgment
of Power, power through control, and control through
power.

For,
there are two sides to every game of conflict.

Through control,
the Pawn is manipulated by the Will power
of the gods-Unseen Hand.

The act of thinking or contemplating upon
one's true nature of self, is profane within
the mind and body of a scriptural god demands
total devotional obedience through unquestionable praise.
The Peasant,
I mean Pawn;
excuse my lack of flattery,
is bound to infinity through its
association with the Cube.

Saturn appears once again dressed in black.

Eight is the expression of the *Noble Truth*,
but the truth is also the hardest nature to bare.

A Pawn exists to serve its master,
and thus,
even though he/she may end up on
the relatively perceived winning side,
the pawn can never win the game, nor
change its status upon the board-a pawn
remains a pawn.

A questionable birth,
leading to a predestined fate.

Is life fair?
Again,
universal balance is impartial,
and thus it is a question that lacks
an answer, beyond karmic influence.

The square is a cross,
a sacrifice demanded by the game.

Now,
oppositionally viewed,
the combined Peasants form the symbolic
Arcane Tower of Mars, and in its Divided expression,
Two Cubes-Black and White.

When these two sacrificial Crosses come
together upon the battlefield of Jerusalem,
the *Double Cross* should become blatantly
clear within the mind of the righteous.

For the *Adept*,
The Esoteric equation:
The Battle of the TWO TOWERS;
 Strength (The Infinite 8+ White peasants)
+ (the Infinite 8- Black pawns) manifests
The Magician and The Lovers/Brothers (Cain and Abel).

Hidden in plain sight,
the unseen is the Eye of the fallen Son,
Phaethon–the Chariot.

I remember a myth,
so to speak,
of a Son of the Sun–the *Shining* One.

Not to be confused with an allegorical tale,
so to speak,
of a Serpent/Nachash that would charm the
lady of the EVEning into conceiving its seed,
bringing forth a *Marked* Child, or maybe
confusion is to be applied.

This Greek Son of Helios,
a *Prince* by design and a charioteer
by Divine inheritance, would *Fall*
from the Heavens by the Will of *Lightning*.

Strange in the Pawn's mind,
it may be,
that another so-called *Shining* One
would also fall from the heavens
with the Will of Lightning.

I could speak of Morning Stars,
but it is just all too familiar.

I will say,
in the interest of the hollow follower,
cover your eyes and fill yourself with
the understanding you are lacking.

Every Sunday or day attributed to the Sun,
you enter the womb of the daughter Saturn–Mother Ceres,
and praise the Father/Son, hypnotically energizing the
harmony and rhythm of His Organ–*Hieros Gamos*.

The Temple of Innana,
where enchanted upright animals,
offer themselves as a sacrifice in the
devotion of Her Son– Tammuz.

Jesus, did I right that?

In the presence of the Holy Spirit,
they euphorically call out Praise *JESUS*! But,
I think it is more correctly pronounced in
Spanish since there is no letter 'J' in Hebrew– *Hesus!*

English translation,
Hail Zeus/Iesous!

Wait a minute,
isn't Zeus the Son of Saturn,
and isn't his symbolic Will a *Lightning* Bolt?

I hear Sherlock Homes in my ear–it's elementary.

I should also mention that Saturn,
in the ancient world, was considered a Sun.
Anyways,
back on track.

Man was created on the 6th day,
and thus the structure of the Pawn
or Cube is six-sided.

When the 3-dimensional Cube is unfolded,
its interior becomes a *Cross*.

Noteworthy is the fact that the Star of David,
Seal of Solomon,
is the ancient symbol of Saturn, hence why
his followers worship him on Saturn's day,
Saturday being the 6th day of the week.

Two more 6's,
and we'll have three of a kind,
isn't Saturn a Triune God?

Saturn is the God of Space/Time and Law,
or chaos and order.

The Pawn is subject to the Law of Motion,
motion, of course,
being the chaos of existence.

Although the Pawn is the most powerful piece
through its number upon the sacrificial field of action,
it is also contradictively the weakest due to
the seemingly unfair advantage its higher-ranked
elements have over it, for strangely, the Pawn is the
only character that cannot move backwards.

Thus,
the Pawn is forced to act without questioning.

Its role is not to think,
but to obey, for contemplation
and reflection is the ability to *step back*
and observe Cause and Effect.

In life,
the unaware Pawn only experiences the illusion of choice,
for the Pawn is subject to only move forward,
and thus through predetermined programming,
is subject to the controlled cycle of space/time.

Interestingly,
the only time the pawn can break its forward Law of motion,
is when it kills.

So its only respite from the repetitious role its
character unwarily plays, is to Kill or be Killed.

Not to mention the way it must kill.
It can be straightforward and true,
or diagonally deceitful.

Its only way to momentarily escape its
predestined fate is to betray itself, by
killing its own reflection—dynamic opposition.

Instead of embracing one's Shadow,
the Pawn is forced through ignorance
to slay its chance of transcendence.

The dimensions of the battlefield are Infinite,
but relatively calculated as 8 x 8 = 64.

The Emperor who rules over the Lovers/Brothers for
Eternity, within the earthly garden of the Fallen
10th Sphere.

Again the hidden Hand is revealed by its equation.

Six,
the symbolic seal being the number of Man,
but Lower man in the IMAGE of his Elohim
Jehovah/Saturn, or more descriptively in nature as the
Demiurge—Yaldabaoth.

Four,
the electromagnetic elemental foundation of sacrifice,
upon which chaos and order bind the Spirit within a vessel
of ignorance, cursed It to repetitiously unwarily play a role
in a Samsaric game that can never be won.

The Ritualistic floor is always Checkered.

The pieces of earthly existence are all represented.

The Pawn; the enslaved people.
The Rook; The Politicians.
The Knight; The Enforcers.
The Bishop; The Priests.
The King; The Judge/Death.
The Queen; Life.

Esoterically speaking,
The Rook,
Knight,
Bishop,
King and Queen are all Aspects,
or potential bodies of the Pawn.

The Rook is the Chariot;
the physical body,
or the Carnal body.

The Knight is the Horse,
the Astral body.

The Bishop is the Driver;
the Mental Body.

The King & Queen represent
the Divine, or Causal Body.

Body–Emotion–Mind–Conscious Will.

Within a state of Ignorance, the Pawn
is only connected to the Physical Body.

Through knowledge of the Body, comes
understanding of the E-motions.

Understanding Emotion raises awareness
of Mind, and with focused, mindful stillness,
Conscious Will is awakened.

The Game cannot be won;
this is an illusion of the ignorant.

What has been forgotten,
is that a Game is not about winning or losing;
it is merely about playing–its simplicity escapes you,
for the ego holds the reins tightly.

This is a sphere of dual perception,
the circle that has been divided and
squared–a 'Circular Plane.'

Understand this, and all contradiction becomes a Unified truth.

The question that lacks an ending, begins with the Answer. "To seek, is not to find, for that which is sought by the seeker, is that which is seeking." –